C000227016

SCOTLAND'S NI

Traverse Theatre Company

Nova Scotia

by John Byrne

cast in order of appearance

Corky Doyle	Nicholas Karimi
Phil McCann	Paul Morrow
Deirdre Chance (aka Didi)	Meg Fraser
Nancy Rice	Cara Kelly
George 'Spanky' Farrell	Gerry Mulgrew
Lucille Bentley	Gerda Stevenson
Miles	Robin Laing

Director	Paddy Cunneen
Designer	Michael Taylor
Lighting Designer	Jeanine Davies
Sound Designer	Euan McLaren
Costume Designers	John Byrne & Aileen Sherry
Wardrobe Supervisor	Sarah Holland

Stage Managers	Hazel Price & Gary Morgan
Deputy Stage Manager	Yvonne Carruthers
Assistant Stage Manager	Tracey Farrell

**first performed at the Traverse Theatre,
Friday 25 April 2008**

a Traverse Theatre Commission

THE TRAVERSE

Artistic Director Dominic Hill

A Rolls-Royce machine for promoting
new Scottish drama across Europe and beyond.
(The Scotsman)

The Traverse's commissioning process embraces a spirit of innovation and risk-taking that has launched the careers of many of Scotland's best-known writers including John Byrne, David Greig, David Harrower and Liz Lochhead. It is unique in Scotland in that it fulfils the crucial role of providing the infrastructure, professional support and expertise to ensure the development of a dynamic theatre culture for Scotland.

The importance of the Traverse is difficult
to overestimate . . . without the theatre, it is difficult
to imagine Scottish playwriting at all. (Sunday Times)

From its conception in the 1960s, the Traverse has remained a pivotal venue during the Edinburgh Festival. It receives enormous critical and audience acclaim for its programming, as well as regularly winning awards. From 2001–07, Traverse Theatre productions of *Gagarin Way* by Gregory Burke, *Outlying Islands* by David Greig, *Iron* by Rona Munro, *The People Next Door* by Henry Adam, *Shimmer* by Linda McLean, *When the Bulbul Stopped Singing* by Raja Shehadeh, *East Coast Chicken Supper* by Martin J Taylor, *Strawberries in January* by Evelyne de la Chenelière in a version by Rona Munro and *Damascus* by David Greig have won Fringe First or Herald Angel awards (and occasionally both).

In 2007 the Traverse's Festival programme *Faithful* picked up an incredible 12 awards including Fringe First awards for Tim Crouch's *ENGLAND* (a Traverse commission) and the Traverse Theatre production of *Damascus* by David Greig, plus a Herald Archangel for outgoing Artistic Director Philip Howard's 'consistent and lasting contribution to Edinburgh's Festivals'.

The Traverse Theatre has established itself as
Scotland's leading exponent of new writing, with
a reputation that extends worldwide. (The Scotsman)

The Traverse's success isn't limited to the Edinburgh stage. Since 2001 Traverse productions of *Gagarin Way, Outlying Islands, Iron, The People Next Door, When the Bulbul Stopped Singing,* the *Slab Boys Trilogy, Mr Placebo* and *Helmet* have toured not only within Scotland and the UK, but in Sweden, Norway, the Balkans, Germany, USA,

Iran, Jordan and Canada. Immediately following the 2006 festival, the Traverse's production of *Petrol Jesus Nightmare #5 (In the Time of the Messiah)* by Henry Adam was invited to perform at the International Festival in Priština, Kosovo and won the Jury Special Award for Production. This spring, the Traverse will tour its award winning 2007 production of *Damascus* to Toronto, New York and Moscow.

One of Europe's most important homes for new plays.
(Sunday Herald)

The Traverse's work with young people is of supreme importance and takes the form of encouraging playwriting through its flagship education project *Class Act*, as well as the Young Writers' Group. *Class Act* is now in its 19th year and gives pupils the opportunity to develop their plays with professional playwrights and work with directors and actors to see the finished piece performed on stage at the Traverse. Last year, for the fourth year running, the project also took place in Russia. The hugely successful Young Writers' Group is open to new writers aged 18–25 and the fortnightly meetings are led by a professional playwright.

In Autumn 2008 the Traverse will, for the first time, work with young men from HM Young Offenders Institution Polmont to improve their literacy skills through practical drama and playwriting. The participants will work with theatre professionals to develop their own plays which will be performed both at HM YOI Polmont and at the Traverse.

The Traverse has an unrivalled reputation for producing contemporary theatre of the highest quality, invention and energy, and for its dedication to new writing. (Scotland on Sunday)

The Traverse is committed to working with international playwrights and, in 2005, produced *In the Bag* by Wang Xiaoli in a version by Ronan O'Donnell, the first ever full production of a contemporary Chinese play in the UK. This project was part of the successful Playwrights in Partnership scheme, which unites international and Scottish writers, and brings the most dynamic new global voices to the Edinburgh stage. Other international Traverse partnerships have included work in Québec, Norway, Finland, France, Italy, Portugal and Japan

www.traverse.co.uk

To find out about ways in which you can support the work of the Traverse please contact our Development Department 0131 228 3223 or development@traverse.co.uk

Charity No. SC002368

COMPANY BIOGRAPHIES

John Byrne (Writer/Costume Designer)
John Byrne was born in Paisley in 1940. He worked as a 'slab boy' at A F Stoddard, the carpet manufacturers, before going to Glasgow School of Art. He became a full time painter in 1968 following his first London exhibition. John is also a distinguished theatre designer and playwright. Previous plays include *The Slab Boys, Cuttin' a Rug, Still Life, Writer's Cramp, Normal Service, Cara Coco* and *Colquhoun and Macbryde*. On television he is best known for his BAFTA Award-winning series *Tutti Frutti* (recently adapted for the stage by National Theatre of Scotland, UK Tour). He has also designed productions for the Traverse Theatre, 7:84, Hampstead Theatre, Bush Theatre and Scottish Opera.

Paddy Cunneen (Director)
Paddy's directing credits include the Chinese Opera *Slippery Mountain in Soho* (Not So Loud Theatre Company); *The Tempest* (Tron Theatre); *Closer* (National Theatre, Lyttleton/European Tour); *His Lordship's Fancy* (Notting Hill Gate); *54% Acrylic, Eye Of The Needle*, Alasdair Gray's *Midgieburgers*, and his own play *Fleeto* (all at Oran Mor), in addition to productions at The Liverpool Everyman, Druid and The Gate. He has worked extensively as a composer and music director in theatre companies throughout the UK and Ireland and is an associate director of Cheek by Jowl. Credits for his music work run to some 180 productions for the National Theatre, RSC, Cheek by Jowl, Out Of Joint, and many others. Work on Broadway includes music for Martin McDonagh's *Beauty Queen of Leenane*; *The Lonesome West*, and *The Pillowman*; plus *The Iceman Cometh, The Blue Room, Private Lives* and *Closer*. Paddy is a recipient of the Christopher Whelen Award for Music in Theatre, and a Critics' Award for Theatre in Scotland for Music (*Twelfth Night*, Dundee Rep). He won the Music Industry Award for Best Cast Album for the Donmar Warehouse production of *Company*. He also composes for radio, has a number of TV and film credits and is BAFTA nominated for his recent score for the Channel 4 film *Boy A*. Two of his plays, *Sunburst Finish* (with Andrea Gibb) and *Disenchantment*, were broadcast on BBC Radio, and a third, *Fleeto*, will tour Scotland in September 2008. In addition to running The Sirens Of Titan community choir, he is proud to have been awarded the 2007 Golden Pie for Best Director at Oran Mor.

Jeanine Davies (Lighting Designer)
For the Traverse: numerous productions including *Hanging the President, Hardy and Baird, Light in the Village*. Theatre credits include *The Unconquered* (Stellar Quines, UK and International Tour, nominated

for 2007 Critics Award for Theatre in Scotland for Best Design).
Jeanine works regularly for a number of theatre companies in her
native Scotland including Citizens Theatre, Dundee Rep, Communicado
and the National Theatre of Scotland as well as The Royal Lyceum in
Edinburgh for whom she is about to light *Trumpets and Raspberries*.
She lit *Tom's Midnight Garden* which opened London's new Unicorn
Theatre. Other theatre credits include *The BFG* (West End); *Rat Pack
Confidential* (West End/Nottingham Playhouse); *The Broken Heart*
(Royal Shakespeare Company); *Cat On A Hot Tin Roof* (UK tour) and
productions at many of England's leading repertory companies. She
also works regularly in Opera and Dance including productions at
the Royal Opera House Linbury Studio and for Scottish Opera, Dance
Base, Classical Opera and X Factor Dance Company. She will also
shortly be working with Fidget Feet Dance Company in Eire, Plan B
Dance Company and the Hebrides Ensemble.

Meg Fraser (Deirdre Chance aka Didi)
Meg trained at RSAMD and was a member of Dundee Rep Ensemble
for 3 years. She was recently been awarded the 2007 TMA Best
Supporting Actress Award for her performance in *All My Sons* (Royal
Lyceum Theatre, Edinburgh) and the 2007 Critics' Award for Theatre
in Scotland, Best Female Performance for her performance in *Tom
Fool* (Citizens Theatre). Other theatre credits include *The Night Before
Christmas* (Coventry Belgrade); *Being Norwegian* (Paines Plough/
Oran Mor); *Game Theory* (Ek Productions); *What I Heard About Iraq*
(James Seabright/Paul Lucas Productions); *Eric Laure* (RSC/Soho
Theatre); *Twelfth Night, As You Like It, Hamlet, Macbeth* (RSC); *Julius
Caesar, The Taming of the Shrew, The Playboy of the Western World*
(Royal Lyceum Theatre, Edinburgh); *The Winter's Tale, Mince* (Dundee
Rep). Radio credits include *An Expert in Murder, The Tenderness of
Wolves, The Trick is to Keep Breathing* (BBC).

Nicholas Karimi (Corky Doyle)
Nicholas trained at Rose Bruford College and graduated in 2005.
For the Traverse: *The Pearlfisher, Seven Miles from Fortune City*
(Rehearsed Reading). Other theatre credits include *Mother Courage*
(Benchtours); *The Dead Fiddler* (New End Theatre); *Mountain Language*
(BAC); *The Emperor Jones* (Gate Theatre); *The Country Wife* (Stephen
Joseph Theatre); *This Here Now* (Royal Lyceum Youth Theatre, Tour).

Cara Kelly (Nancy Rice)
Cara trained at RSAMD and won the 2006 Critics' Award for Theatre
in Scotland for her performance in *Molly Sweeney*, the Carleton Hobbs
Radio 4 Award and the James Bridie Gold Medal while at RSAMD.
Theatre credits include *Molly Sweeney, Shadow of a Gunman,
Blood Wedding, Romeo and Juliet, The Borrowers* (Citizens Theatre);

Henry VIII (RSC); *Elizabeth Gordon Quinn* (National Theatre of Scotland/Royal Lyceum Theatre/Citizens Theatre); *Anna Karenina, Juno and the Paycock, Ghosts* (Royal Lyceum Theatre, Edinburgh); *Top Girls* (New Vic, Stoke); *On Raftery's Hill* (Druid); *The Steward of Christendom* (Gate Theatre, Dublin) *King Lear, All Things Nice, Loyal Women,* (Royal Court); *Translations* (Donmar Warehouse); *The Life of Galileo* (Almeida Theatre); *Playboy of the Western World, Therese Raquin* (Communicado); *You Never Can Tell* (West Yorkshire Playhouse); *The Winter's Tale, Miss Julie* (Young Vic). Television credits include *Sunday* (Channel 4); *Taggart* (SMG); *Holy Cross, State of Play, Life Support, The Precious Blood, Monarch of the Glen, River City, Bramwell, Ultimate Force, Dr Finlay* (BBC); *Superintendent Winter, Between the Lines, The Bill* (ITV).

Robin Laing (Miles)
Theatre credits include *Living Quarters, The Winter's Tale, Monks, All My Sons, As You Like It* (Royal Lyceum Theatre, Edinburgh); *Mary Stuart, Elizabeth Gordon Quinn* (National Theatre of Scotland/Royal Lyceum Theatre/Citizens Theatre); *Slope* (Untitled Projects/Tramway); *Invention of Love* (Salisbury Playhouse); *Medea* (Abbey Theatre/ Broadway, Paris Tour); *A Midsummer Night's Dream, Loot* (Manchester Royal Exchange); *The Mill Lavvies* (Dundee Rep); *Skylight* (Perth Theatre); *Trainspotting* (UK Tour/West End). Television credits include *Taggart* (SMG); *Murder City* (Granada); *Born and Bred, Waking the Dead, Into the Blue, The Lakes, Murder Rooms: The Dark Beginnings of Sherlock Holmes* (BBC); *Band of Brothers* (HBO/Dreamworks). Film credits include *Joyeux Noel* (Nord Ouest Productions); *Joy Rider* (Classic Film Production); *Borstal Boy* (Hell's Kitchen); *Beautiful Creatures* (DNA). Robin played the role of Phil McCann in the film version of *The Slab Boys* (Skreba Films).

Euan McLaren (Sound Designer)
Euan has been Deputy Electrician at the Traverse since 2005 with special responsibility for sound and video. During his time at the Traverse Euan has worked on productions that have toured Canada, Jordan, Russia and the USA. He previously worked at the **mac**robert and Pitlochry Festival Theatre.

Paul Morrow (Phil McCann)
Paul trained at RSAMD in Glasgow graduating with the Citizens Prize. For the Traverse: *Just Frank, Buchanan.* Recent theatre credits include *God's Hairdresser, Targets, The Price of a Fish Supper* (Oran Mor); *Great Expectations, Sunset Song* (Prime Productions); *The Demon Barber* (Perth Theatre); *The Bevellers* (Citizens Theatre); *Writers Cramp* (Royal Lyceum Theatre, Edinburgh); *Two Weeks With*

The Queen (Visible Fictions). Paul has appeared in many television programmes, including *Taggart, Monarch of the Glen, Winners and Losers* and the BAFTA award winning film *The Long Roads*. He has also worked extensively as a voice-over artist and has performed in numerous radio plays.

Gerry Mulgrew (George 'Spanky' Farrell)
Gerry has worked in the theatre for 30 years, variously as an actor, director, writer and musician. He is perhaps best known as the artistic director of Communicado, a company he co-founded in 1983. The company has produced over 30 distinct theatre shows including *Cyrano De Bergerac, The Cone Gatherers, Blood Wedding, Mary Queen Of Scots Got Her Head Chopped Off, Brave* and *Zlata's Diary*. In addition to touring all over Scotland, from Shetland to the Borders, Communicado has also performed work in the USA, Canada, Turkey, Egypt and throughout Europe. As an actor Gerry has performed with many theatres in Scotland and most recently played Old Peer Gynt in *Peer Gynt* (Dundee Rep/National Theatre of Scotland) and Vladimir in *Waiting for Godot* (Citizens Theatre). Gerry has also worked extensively as a director and his work has been seen across the UK, including many venues in London and the Royal Shakespeare Company. For the past two years he has also been directing in Madrid and East Africa. Recently, he adapted and directed Robin Jenkins' *Fergus Lamont* (Communicado), directed *An Everyday Occurrence* (Mr McFall's Chamber) and directed *Mactalla Nan Eun (The Echo of Birds)*, a Gaelic music theatre piece performed at the Gaelic Arts Project in Stornnoway. This was presented as part of the Pan European Project which saw the same script being performed simultaneously in five different countries.

Aileen Sherry (Costume Design)
Aileen has worked in Scottish theatre since 2000 as a costume supervisor and designer/maker. For the Traverse: the *Slab Boys Trilogy, The Found Man, In the Bag, One Day All This Will Come To Nothing, Damascus, The Pearlfisher*. Aileen has also worked with Scottish Youth Theatre, Citizens Theatre, Tron Theatre, Byre Theatre, Prime Productions, Out of Joint, King's Panto Glasgow, National Theatre of Scotland and Scottish Opera. Film credits include *The Jacket* (Warner Independent Pictures) and *Nina's Heavenly Delights* (Kali Films).

Gerda Stevenson (Lucille Bentley)
Gerda trained at RADA. Theatre credits include *Frozen* (Rapture Theatre - Best Female Performance nomination Critics Awards for Theatre in Scotland, 2007); *The Yellow on the Broom* (Perth Repertory

Theatre); *Zlata's Diary, The Suicide, A Place with the Pigs, Jock Tamson's Bairns* (Communicado); *Phaedra, Dancing at Lughnasa, Tartuffe, A Streetcar Named Desire, Hobson's Choice, Othello* (Royal Lyceum Theatre, Edinburgh); *The Meeting* (Edinburgh International Festival); *And The Cow Jumped Over The Moon, Anna Campbell* (Traverse Theatre); *Night Sky* (Stellar Quines); *A Wee Bit of How Do You Do* (Sounds of Progress). Television credits include: *Heartbeat* (ITV Yorkshire); *Midsomer Murders* (Bentley Productions); *The Bill* (Thames TV); *Life Support, Rough Justice, The High Life, River City,* (BBC); *The Boyhood of John Muir* (PBS, USA). Film credits include *How D'Yae Want to Die?* (Dead Man's Shoes Productions); *Swinefever* (Hart Fever); *Braveheart* (Marquis Films); *Blue Black Permanent* (Viz Films - Scottish BAFTA Best Film Actress). Gerda has worked extensively in radio and currently plays Steve Temple in *The Paul Temple Mysteries* (BBC Radio 4). She is also a director and writer. Her radio dramatisation of Scott's epic novel *The Heart of Midlothian,* in which she played the heroine Jeanie Deans, is nominated for the 2008 Sony Awards. Gerda has directed widely in theatre, opera, film and radio, most recently at Oran Mor, Glasgow. She was the founder of Stellar Quines, and is Associate Director of Communicado Theatre Company. www.gerdastevenson.co.uk

Michael Taylor (Designer)
Michael trained as a designer at RADA. His work includes *The Clean House* (National Tour 2008); *Living Quarters, All My Sons, Les Liaisons Dangereuses, Death of a Salesman* (Royal Lyceum Theatre, Edinburgh); *In Extremis* (Shakespeare's Globe); *Clever Dick, Out in the Open, Keepers, The Awakening, Four Door Saloon, My Boy Jack* (Hampstead Theatre); *Shadow of a Gunman, John Bull's Other Island* (Tricycle); *Private Lives* and *Present Laughter* (Theatre Royal Bath, Tour); *Lies Have Been Told* (New End and Trafalgar Studios); *Men Should Weep, Easter* (Oxford Stage Company, Tour); *Amphibians* (RSC); *Mountain Language* (world premiere written and directed by Harold Pinter, RNT); *Rafts and Dreams* (Royal Court); *Darwin in Malibu, No Sweat* (Birmingham Rep); *Vita and Virginia* (Altes Schauspielhaus, Stuttgart); (Hampstead Theatre); *The Pool at Bethesda* (Guildhall); *The Fatherland, Millfire* (Riverside Studios); *The Road to Nirvana* (Traverse/ King's Head); *Death of a Salesman* (York Theatre Royal); *Time and the Conways, Ragdoll* (Bristol Old Vic); and productions at the Bush, Royal Exchange, Sheffield Crucible, Nottingham Playhouse and elsewhere.

SPONSORSHIP AND DEVELOPMENT

We would like to thank the following
corporate funders for their support

Scottish & Newcastle UK

LUMISON

To find out how you can benefit
from being a Traverse Corporate Funder,
please contact our Development Department
on 0131 228 3223 / development@traverse.co.uk

**The Traverse would like to thank
the members of the Development Board:**

Stewart Binnie, Adrienne Sinclair Chalmers,
Stephen Cotton, Paddy Scott and Ian Wittet

**The Traverse Theatre's work
would not be possible without the support of**

**The Traverse Theatre receives
financial assistance from:**

The Barcapel Foundation The Binks Trust,
The Calouste Gulbenkian Foundation,
The Canadian High Commission, The Craignish Trust,
The Cross Trust, The Cruden Foundation,
Gouvernement de Québec,
James Thom Howat Charitable Trust,
The Japan Foundation, The John Thaw Foundation,
The Lloyds TSB Foundation for Scotland,
The Misses Barrie Charitable Trust,
The Moffat Charitable Trust,
The Peggy Ramsay Foundation,
Ronald Duncan Literary Foundation,
Sky Youth Action Fund, Tay Charitable Trust,
The Thistle Trust, The Weatherall Foundation

**For their continued generous support
of Traverse productions,
the Traverse thanks:**

The Pier, 104 George Street, Edinburgh;
Habitat;
Marks and Spencer, Princes Street;
Camerabase

**For their help on _Nova Scotia_,
the Traverse thanks:**

Niamh O'Meara, Pitlochry Festival Theatre,
National Theatre of Scotland, Royal Lyceum Theatre,
Tron Theatre, Citizens Theatre, The Warehouse,
Pilton Video, Blimey Productions, Inch Nursery,
Bunting and Great Great Auntie Sadie

Charity No. SC002368

ARE YOU DEVOTED?

Our Devotees are: Joan Aitken, Stewart Binnie, Katie Bradford, Adrienne Sinclair Chalmers, Adam Fowler, Anne Gallacher, Keith Guy, Iain Millar, Helen Pitkethly, Michael Ridings, Bridget Stevens, Walton & Parkinson

The Traverse could not function without the generous support of our patrons. In March 2006 the Traverse Devotees was launched to offer a whole host of exclusive benefits to our loyal supporters.

Become a Traverse Devotee for £29 per month or £350 per annum and receive:

- A night at the theatre including six tickets, drinks and a backstage tour

- Your name inscribed on a brick in our wall

- Sponsorship of one of our brand new Traverse 2 seats

- Invitations to Devotees' events

- Your name featured on this page in Traverse Theatre Company scripts and a copy mailed to you

- Free hire of the Traverse Bar Café (subject to availability)

Bricks in our wall and seats in Traverse 2 are also available separately. Inscribed with a message of your choice, these make ideal and unusual gifts.

To join the Devotees or to discuss giving us your support in another way, please contact our Development Department on 0131 228 3223 / development@traverse.co.uk

TRAVERSE THEATRE – THE COMPANY

Andy Catlin	Marketing Manager
Laura Collier	Associate Producer
Lindsey Dawson	Finance Manager
Maureen Deacon	Finance Assistant
Steven Dickson	Head Chef
Neil Donachie	Bar Café Duty Manager
Sandra Dow	Development Assistant
Martin Duffield	Box Office Manager
Claire Elliot	Assistant Electrician
Craig Fyfe	Commis Chef
Mike Griffiths	Administrative Director
Gavin Harding	Production Manager
Dominic Hill	Artistic Director
Aimee Johnstone	Bar Café Assistant Manager
Kath Lowe	Front of House Manager
Norman Macleod	Development Manager
Euan McLaren	Deputy Electrician
Katherine Mendelsohn	Literary Manager
Sarah Murray	Administrative Assistant
Noëlle O'Donoghue	Learning & Participation Officer
Gwen Orr	Theatre Manager
Emma Pirie	Press & Marketing Officer
Pauleen Rafferty	Finance & Personnel Assistant
Renny Robertson	Chief Electrician
Aileen Sherry	Wardrobe Supervisor
Steven Simpson	Executive Bar Café Manager
Louise Stephens	Literary Assistant
Phil Turner	Technical Stage Manager
Liz Wallace	Marketing & Press Assistant
Alan Wilkins	Young Writers Group Leader

Also working for the Traverse

Peter Airlie, Peter Boyd, Hannah Cornish, Koralia Daskalaki, Oliver Dimelow, Dan Dixon, Morag Donnachie, Perrie Dunnett, Julie Eveleigh, Marianne Forde, Andrew Gannon, Linda Gunn, Zophie Horsted, Thomas Hutchinson, Neil Johnstone, Tessa Kelly, Jennifer Kempton, Rebecca King, Anna Kulikowska, Terry Leddy, Kate Leiper, Graeme Mackie, Heather Marshall, Jon-James McGregor, Adam Millar, John Mitchell, Ewa Nagraba, Grant Neave, Niamh O'Meara, Matthew Ozga-Lawn, Clare Padgett, Michael Ramsay, Emma Robertson, Greg Sinclair, Caitlin Skinner, Caroline Spence, Naomi Stalker, David Taylor, Emma Taylor, Ailsa Thomson, Imogen Toner, Nick Torpy, Anna Walsh, Jenna Watt, Katie Wilson.

TRAVERSE THEATRE BOARD OF DIRECTORS

Stephen Cotton (Chair), Adrienne Sinclair Chalmers (Company Secretary), Lynne Crossan, Susan Deacon, Chris Hannan, Caroline Gardner, Sheila Murray, Margaret Waterston.

John Byrne
Nova Scotia

with illustrations by the author

faber and faber

First published in 2008
by Faber and Faber Limited
3 Queen Square, London WC1N 3AU

Typeset by Country Setting, Kingsdown, Kent CT14 8ES
Printed in England by CPI Bookmarque, Croydon, Surrey

A CIP record for this book
is available from the British Library

ISBN 978–0–571–24264–1

2 4 6 8 10 9 7 5 3 1

Characters

Corky Doyle

Phil McCann

Didi Chance

Nancy Rice

George (Spanky) Farrell

Lucille Farrell

Miles McCann

NOVA SCOTIA

Act One

The neglected garden and grounds of a fortified house in the far north-east of Scotland. Part of the back of the house, plus part of a modern extension, butts on from stage left. Refectory table with debris from the previous evening's alfresco supper stage centre-ish, scattering of chairs, together with kiddies' outdoor toys, e.g. space-hopper, pram, pedal car.

A summer's morning in the early years of the new millennium.

A young man, Corky Doyle, sporting long hair and a little chin-beard, appears round side of house carrying flight cases. He surveys garden and grounds before dumping flight cases on grass and disappearing back the way he came.

As Corky leaves, Phil McCann appears, crawling slowly on all fours from under table, obviously badly hungover. He is in his sixties. Crawls towards house, managing with some effort to get himself onto his pins, peeling crumpled shirt off and negotiating minefield of playthings before disappearing inside house.

Sound of van taking off from front of house as Corky reappears with more flight cases, etc. He dumps these and rolls joint from last of papers and tobacco on refectory table. Parks roll-up behind his ear and stands with eyes closed, feeling the 'vibes'.

Phil reappears, pulling a fresh shirt over his head and in some miraculous way avoiding barking his shins on the playthings strewing the garden. Eventually his head emerges bleary-eyed from shirt collar.

Phil (*spotting Corky*) Oh.

Corky (*turning to look*) Ah. Cool shurt, man.

Phil Sorry, thought you wur goin' to be . . .

Corky Late? Not on yur life . . . That was the old Corky Doyle, you're lookin' at the newly minted Corky Doyle. (*Sticking hand out.*) Corky Doyle.

Phil takes his hand.

Nice place you got here . . . Didi described it as fifteenth-century, but I'm pretty sure that crenellation work up there goes way back to . . . Holy Christ, man, what is that?!

Phil (*turning to follow his gaze*) What?

Corky *That there.* It's like strollin' nonchalantly round the back of the Rokeby Venus only to discover she's got this monstrous great plook on hur arse. What is it, some sorta old folks' sun-lounge area?

Phil That's my studio.

Corky (*making camera frame with hands*) What was this joint 'fore you lot moved in, a residential home, yeh?

Phil How come you two are acquainted?

Corky Sorry?

Phil You and Deirdre.

Corky Who?

Phil You mentioned *Didi* earlier on when you were –

Corky (*overlapping*) Aw, er . . . yeh . . .

Telephone rings indoors.

We've, uh . . . we've talked on the tele— Fuckin hell!

He ducks low as a jet fighter screams over rooftop.

8

PHIL

9

Phil (*unfazed*) You might want to set yur recordin' gear up inside before they start firing thur hippy-seekin' missiles.

He moves off to house to answer phone. Corky, perplexed, looks up at the sky. As Phil disappears into house, we hear a Cherokee jeep draw up out front. Didi appears round side of house. She tiptoes across to table, glances underneath, rushes across to Corky and throws her arms around him.

Corky (*startled*) Waaaaah!

Didi God, I've missed you!

Corky Same here.

They kiss passionately. Didi breaks off, breathless.

Didi I was terrified I was going to arrive and find the pair of you getting on like a house on fire . . . (*They kiss.*) Must've gone to the garage for tobacco . . . (*They kiss.*)

Corky (*breaking off, breathless*) He's jist went to answer the phone . . .

Didi (*as Corky makes to kiss her again*) What?

Corky C'mere.

Didi You must be joking . . . He'll kill me!

Beats a hasty retreat just as Phil appears from house.

Phil Thought you said you were from the wireless?

Corky Wireless?

Phil I've jist been givin' Nancy what's-her-name directions on hur mobile, says she's never heard of you.

Corky That's funny, 'cos I've never heard of hur either.

He picks up digital movie camera from case.

Phil What the bloody hell is that?

Corky (*pointing camera at Phil*) Music video, man.

Phil Music *what-eo*?

Didi reappears round side of house, laden down with groceries. Corky swings round to get her in his sights.

Didi Hullo? I'm back! God, what a glorious day. (*Loudly.*) I hope you're not still lying spark out under that table?

Peeping round grocery bags, she spots Corky as though for first time.

Oh, hi, you must be Cooky.

Corky *Corky* . . . Hi. (*Lowering camera.*) Here, lemme grab some of those.

Didi Oh, would you? Thanks.

Phil I'll get them.

Shoulders Corky aside, takes bags from Didi.

Jeesus.

Didi (*to Corky*) You managed to find us . . . I'm impressed.

Phil Well, don't be, he's just leavin' . . . D'you manage to get ma rollin' tobacco?

Corky (*peering round camera, to Phil*) D'you want to shift that way a tad? Then yur outta frame . . . Cheers. (*Framing up on Didi.*) Nice one, yeh.

Phil Listen, you, whatever-yur-bloody-name-is, if you urny off ma property in two seconds flat, I swear to God . . .

Corky (*crabbing round Didi*) You've done this before, huven't you? I can tell . . . Woooow.

Phil Right, that's it. (*Dumps groceries.*) Give us that bloody gadget . . .

He makes a breenge at Corky.

Corky Hey, whoa . . . Cool it, old timer.

Phil What'd you jist call us? (*Another breenge.*) Gimme that!

Didi (*intervening, to Phil*) Oh, for God's sake, behave! Stop that . . . stop it! I told you all about this shoot and it's not *your* property, it's *mine* . . . (*To Corky.*) Are you okay?

Phil Never heed is he okay . . . You told me about a catalogue shoot for kiddies' wear and you never said it was goin' to be this mornin'. I've got people arrivin' any minute to do an extremely important radio interview which I told you about months ago . . . This clown's talkin' about filmin' a rock concert in the bloody garden!

Didi (*to Corky*) You didn't tell me it was a rock concert. God, how *fabulous*!

Corky (*still fending Phil off*) Don't listen to him, it's just some has-been wi' an acoustic guitar.

Phil I don't give a toss if it's a deaf mute wi' a chocolate banjo, you give me one good reason why hur an' I should let you –

Didi (*overlapping*) We need the money!

Phil stops pawing at Corky, looks daggers at Didi.

We need the money, Phil.

Phil Okay, so we're not exactly *flush* at the moment, but it canny be all that much . . . (*Looking from one to the other and back again.*)

Didi Two and a half grand.

Corky A day.

Didi Over three days.

A jet fighter passes overhead – not quite as screamingly loud this time, but loud enough.

Corky Could take longer.

Phil (*after pause, to Didi*) D'you want a hand to clear that table?

Didi I'll manage.

Phil picks up groceries, Corky gathers some footage on camera. Didi tackles debris from night before's supper.
Nancy Rice, looking like a slightly past-it rock chick in shades and toreador pants, appears round side of house, lugging a bulky shoulder bag. Corky swings into action, weaving in and around her as she crosses the grass.

Nancy Wooo-hooo. (*Punching the air.*) Made it . . . Yo!

Didi crosses from table with trayload of dirty crockery etc. towards house.

Didi (*to Phil, in passing*) I'll fix some coffee, yeh?

Nancy (*coming towards Phil, hand outstretched*) Hey . . . good to meet you.

Phil sets one bag of groceries down and takes hold of Nancy's outstretched hand. Nancy parks shades on top of her head and surveys house and garden.

Phil (*aside, to Corky*) Not too bad shape furra has-been. Toreador pants're a bit of a giveaway. When did she have hur last hit single . . . nineteen fifty-two? (*Picks up other grocery bags. To Nancy.*) Didny happen to run into an old bag wi' a BBC bumper-sticker on the back of hur invalid carriage? (*Setting off for house.*) Canny think how else she could be this late . . .

Mobile phone rings. Corky, still shooting around
Nancy, takes mobile out and clamps it to his ear.

If she turns up in the next ten minutes, give us a shout, yeh?

Nancy I wouldn't have been this late if the map you sent my PA hadn't been drawn up by a five-year-old child on a sheet of corrugated cardboard!

Phil (*turning to Nancy*) He'll not be five till the end of May next year.

Nancy (*briskly*) Nancy Rice, Sony Award Winner for Arts Programming on Scottish Network Radio for the past three consecutive years and runner-up for the Italia Prize in two thousand and two for my documentary feature on *The Graphic Art of Eduardo Paolozzi* for RTE . . . (*Dumping bag.*) You okay for doing it out here? Or d'you want to talk in the lean-to behind you? I'm easy.

Phil That 'lean-to' happens to be my . . .

Corky strolls past on mobile, lets out cackle.

Naw, out here's fine.

As Corky places roll-up in mouth:

I trust that isny a joint you're about to light up. This happens to be a designated play area . . . any child seein' you wi' a spliff's goin' to have it off you. (*To Nancy.*) How d'you take yur coffee?

Nancy sets up DAT recorder and notes. Phil dumps groceries on grass.

Nancy How d'you take yours?

Phil (*loudly, towards house*) Two toddlers' coffees, tonsa sugar, sweetheart!

Nancy makes face. Phil joins her at table.

NANCY

Ready when you are, doll . . . (*Loudly, towards house.*)
I hope you remembered to get me some rollin' tobacco!

Corky (*breaking off call*) In the bag wi' the butter.

*He carries on mumbling into mobile. Phil rootles
around in grocery bag and finds pouch of American
Spirit tobacco.*

Phil (*to himself*) What's the bettin' she never got me any
bloody papers? (*Pause.*) Hang on a second . . .

*Looks at pouch, then at Corky. Didi appears from
house with tray. Nancy dons headset. Corky wanders
to and fro, still on mobile.*

Nancy (*into DAT*) One, two, three, four . . . one, two,
three, four –

*Phil frowns. Didi places tray on table and hands coffee
mug to Nancy, who takes off headset.*

Thanks. (*Takes slug of coffee – chokes.*) Oh, my God!

Didi Let me get you a fruit tea.

Nancy No, no, it was the shock . . . I thought you were
the help. I didn't realise. I'm such a huge fan of yours.
Congratulations, by the way.

Phil Water under the bridge, sweetheart. Different if
she'd won all that dosh.

Nancy (*to Didi*) I know from reading your cuttings you
don't normally do interviews, but if I got my PA to drop
you a line . . .

Phil Yur on a sticky wicket there, honeybunch. Tell us
when yur ready to rock'n'roll. (*To Didi.*) What've you
done with them, if that isny too stupid a question?

Didi They were running rings round me at the
supermarket. I dropped them off at Skelbo on the way

back. Heidi said she was happy to look after them for
a bit . . .

Phil Ma cigarette papers, I'm talkin' about. Six packets
of Silver Rizlas . . .

*Corky punches number into mobile. House phone
rings.*

Didi Excuse me.

*She heads towards house. Nancy dons headset, takes it
off, checks running speed of DAT, puts headset back
on, etc.*

Phil C'mon, you've been footerin' with that contraption
fur ages . . . I could've penned the furst ten chapters of
ma life story while you've been on an' off wi' them
headphones . . .

Nancy Be right with you.

Phil (*to Corky*) Hope you're not goin' to be shoutin' an'
bawlin' into that bloody handset while hur an' I's
recordin'?

Nancy (*into DAT*) Twenty-second trail, Programme Five.

Corky (*into mobile*) Hi, babe, it's me . . . what kept you?
(*Sniggers.*)

Phil glares at Corky.

Nancy (*reading from notes*) How genuine are those
much-publicised claims to alcohol addiction, autism, life-
saving surgery and family insanity put forward by some
of the 'elder statesmen' of Scottish painting over the last
couple of decades . . . or is it all just so much boo-hoo,
poor-me, headline-grabbing PR spewed out in a desperate
bid for much-needed art world *cred* by a bunch of
incontinent, over-the-hill tossers for whom the writing is
so very clearly on the gallery wall? Join me, Nancy Rice,

17

for *The Sweet Smell of Success or the Putrid Stench of Old Tripe?*, a *Nancy Rice Show* special, Friday night at eight, BBC Radio Scotland . . . (*Hits pause button – to Phil.*) Right, d'you want to go for it?

Phil Go for it? You must be jokin', sweetheart! Do you imagine fur one minute that I'm goin' to sit here and . . .

Nancy (*lifting one side of headset*) Sorry, I couldn't hear a word of that.

Phil That is unfortunate because I could hear every word of that trailer. Do you imagine fur one minute that I'm goin' to sit here and –

Corky on mobile lets out loud guffaw.

(*To Corky.*) I've told you once to bugger off. I am not tellin' you again . . . Now, bugger off!

Corky (*into mobile*) Hang on a second . . . (*To Phil.*) D'you mind? I'm tryin' to huv a crucial dialogue here . . . in *private*! (*Into mobile.*) Sorry about that, carry on . . . you wur sayin' . . .

Phil (*turning to Nancy*) Did you hear what he just –?

Nancy (*into mobile*) Message for Barbara . . .

Phil Sufferin' God in heaven . . .

Nancy (*into mobile*) Hi, Babs, could you make out a booking form in the name of Didi Chance . . . dee-eye-dee-eye . . . Hold on . . . (*To Phil.*) What's your partner's job description?

Phil (*head in his hands*) I don't have a partner . . . never even had an apprentice, fur God's sake.

Corky (*into mobile*) Yeh, catch you later, babe. (*Signs off, puts in new number.*)

Nancy No, I mean, how would she describe herself? (*Into mobile.*) Be right with you, Babs.

Phil Aw, I don't know . . . *rangy*? She thinks her feet are enormous. I personally think she's a big ride, but then what do I know? I'm just one of yur incontinent over-the-hill tossers, right?

Nancy You weren't actually meant to be eavesdropping. (*Into mobile.*) Call you back, Barbara . . . Bye.

Phil I could hardly help but *eavesdrop* – I'm sittin' right here, fur Christ's sake . . . Even the throwback in the goatee could hear every word an' he was at the other end of the bloody garden makin' lovey-dovey phone calls to some lassie or other . . . (*To Corky.*) She's obviously never clapped eyes on you yet, whoever she is!

Didi appears from house.

Corky (*into mobile*) Sorry, Miles, the occupier's tryin' to attract ma attention . . . (*To Phil.*) What is it now? I'm talkin' to ma director . . . What? *What?*

Phil God, listen to it . . . Don't you start gettin' narky, pal. I live here, you're just a paying guest worker . . . (*To Didi.*) Who was on the phone?

Didi Oh, er . . . it was . . . it was Heidi . . . She wants me to go and rescue her.

Phil What's she need rescuin' from? That pair wouldny say boo to a goose.

Didi That's all you know. Poor girl sounded terrified.

Corky (*into mobile*) Naw, yur breakin' up, say again?

Didi Absolutely terrified.

Phil What one's Heidi? Lassie wi' the braids?

Didi Not any more, she isn't . . . they found a pair of dressmaking scissors. Right, I'm off. (*Heading for side of house.*) Anyone need anything from the shop, no? Good. Shan't be too long . . . Bye.

She disappears.

Corky (*pocketing mobile*) Anybody know where Skelmo Castle is?

Phil Skel-*bo*, ya dummy. (*Loudly.*) Didi!

Didi (*reappearing*) What?

Phil Got yurself a passenger . . . Don't rush back. Not you, *him*. Oh, an' remember an' get us fag papers this time!

Corky Give us the dough, then.

Phil Not you, *hur*.

Didi Come on if you're coming.

She disappears.

Corky Anybody see a lighter? (*Hunts around.*)

Didi (*off, loudly*) Get a move on, will you?

Corky I've lost ma lucky lighter, dammit!

Didi (*off, loudly*) The babysitter's going to lose what's left of her hair if you don't hurry up! Come on!

Sound of Cherokee revving up out front.

Corky (*nicking book of matches from table, to Phil*) How d'you put up wi' that, man? (*Loudly.*) I'm there already!

Takes off at a gallop round side of house. Silence, save for birdsong, bees and music drifting from house out over garden. Nancy busies herself with writing notes, rubbing out and rewriting. Phil mops his brow.

Phil That bloody butter's goin' to melt.

He wanders across to where he dumped grocery bags, stops en route to pick something up from the grass. It is Corky's lighter.

Didi

Corky Doyle

Phil flicks lighter on and off – then on again. Flame starts to flicker as his hand shakes. Although it's an excessively warm day now, Phil stands there shaking like it's freezing cold. He pockets lighter.

Don't want another coffee, naw?

Without waiting for Nancy's answer, he picks up groceries and disappears into the house.

Nancy runs DAT back to 'for whom the writing is so very clearly on the gallery wall'. She puts headset back on and hits 'record'.

Nancy (*into DAT*) Join me, Nancy Rice, for *The Nancy Rice Show* special where we'll be discussing, not the avant garde but the *old* guard . . . We'll even be talking to one or two of them – first up is Paisley-born Philip McCann, whose diptych 'Mental Health', depicting his mother in a straitjacket being sexually assaulted by what one leading critic described as 'a refugee from *The Black and White Minstrels* got up as a runaway rating from *HMS Pinafore*' with a rolled-up copy of *Psychiatry Today* while the artist looks helplessly on from the sidelines, won him few new friends on the Scottish art scene when it was shown at the RSA's Summer Exhibition . . . thus putting paid to what a great many influential people thought was a promising career as a portrait painter of note. I'll be challenging McCann to defend his right to rub our noses in the public display of private misfortune and looking for answers on other topics such as sex and old age, marriage, children, divorce and death, and – wait for it – the biggest question of all: what does one of our greatest living artists – perhaps the greatest that Scotland has ever produced – see in an old reactionary like him? Friday night at eight, BBC Radio Scotland . . .

Phil reappears from house with fresh mug of coffee and joins Nancy. Nancy hits 'pause' button.

Phil What you playin' at, startin' without me?

Nancy Just making some alterations to that trail you weren't supposed to hear.

Phil (*gratified*) I should bloody well hope so.

Nancy (*checking watch*) Okay, let's do this. (*Starts DAT.*) I'm sitting here on a perfect summer's day with the easel painter Phil McCann in the wildly romantic garden of . . .

Phil (*overlapping*) Hold it, hold it.

Nancy (*hitting 'pause'*) What?

Phil You just described me as an '*easel* painter'.

Nancy So?

Phil I don't paint easels, I paint canvases, hardboard, cardboard, MDF . . .

Nancy Fine, fine . . . let's go again. (*Into DAT.*) I'm sitting here on a perfect summer's day with the oil painter Phil McCann in the wildly –

Phil (*cutting her off*) Quit actin' it . . . *Painter*'s just fine, you don't have to qualify it, modify it, or tittify it in any way whatsoever, right?

Nancy Right! (*Into DAT.*) I'm sitting here on a perfect summer's day with the *painter* Phil McCann in the wildly romantic –

Phil Naw, naw, naw, naw . . . you're hittin' it too hard now . . . It's like sayin', 'I'm sittin' here with the *murderer* Phil McCann.' Do it right or don't do it at all. Honest to Christ . . .

Nancy Here . . .

Removes headset and chucks it at Phil.

Why don't you just interview yourself and be done with it?!

Gets up and moves away from table, stands with her back to Phil.

Phil C'mon, you know exactly what I mean.

Nancy ignores him. Phil ponders for some moments before donning headset. Presses 'rewind' button by mistake. Nancy rounds on him.

Nancy Gimme that!

Reclaims headset and stops DAT.

God, you bloody well would've done too!

Phil What?

Nancy (*dons headset; mimicking Phil*) 'So, tell me, Mr Wonderful, what's it like being me?' 'Aw, shucks, just . . . *wonderful*!'

Phil Get it right, then . . . don't *colour* stuff, that's my job.

Nancy And it's my job to get this in the can before . . . (*Checks watch.*) Shit. Okay, ready? (*Restarts DAT.*) I'm sitting here on a perfect summer's day with the painter Phil McCann in the wildly romantic garden of the fortified house in the far north-east of Scotland that he shares with the celebrated video artist Didi Chance and their two small . . . *bugger.* (*Stops, rewinds.*)

Phil What's up now? That was fine.

Nancy (*listening on headset*) Shhh! (*Into DAT.*) . . . with the celebrated video artist and current Turner Prize nominee Didi Chance and their two small children . . . (*Glancing at notes.*) Hector and Lucky . . . Damn, shit and bugger! (*Hits 'pause', laughs.*) My fault . . . sorry. (*Rewinds – into DAT.*) . . . Hector and *Lucy.* Tell me, Phil, what's it like sharing this house with –

Phil (*overlapping*) You were right the first time.

Nancy (*pausing DAT*) *What?*

Phil It isny 'Lucy', it's –

Nancy You're joking.

Phil I'm not.

Nancy (*laughing*) Lucky *McCann?*

Phil Naw, Lucky *Chance* . . . after hur mother. Carry on.

Nancy (*soberly*) Ah, that's different . . . that's funny in quite a deeply serious way. Let's press on, I can fix the name thing later . . . (*Replacing headset.*) Now . . .

Spanky (*offstage, distant*) Hullo . . . anybody home?

Nancy Tell me, Phil, what's it like sharing this house with one of the year's short-listed artists for the most prestigious and coveted award in contemporary art? Is it a little overwhelming for someone like yourself, whose main claim to fame in recent times has been more to do with a fall from grace than an elevation to the Pantheon of Bearded Worthies who are all too . . .

Spanky (*tilting shades up*) Hi.

Nancy (*startled*) Waaah!

George Farrell, aka Spanky, is dressed in an expensively tailored kaftan-type top over blue jeans and scuffed hand-made loafers, his long grey-gold hair tied back, a drop-earring in his left ear lobe. He is wearing shades and looking all of his sixty-four years despite, or perhaps because of, his Californian tan.

Phil (*failing to recognise the intruder*) What the bloody hell d'you want?

Spanky (*affecting West Coast drawl*) Hey, easy . . . take it easy, man. I obviously got a bum address . . . Is thur a dude cried Miles lives in this neighbourhood? (*Peering at*

Nancy – big smile.) Pardon me, I thought you wur Chrissie Hynde furra second . . .

Phil Nup, doesny ring a bell . . . an' it isny a 'neighbourhood' on account of how we huvny any neighbours . . . (*To Nancy.*) Sorry, what wur you askin' me? I wasny really listenin', to be honest.

Nancy (*restarting DAT*) I was asking what it felt like sharing this house with one of –

Phil (*to Spanky, who is nosing around*) I realise it might be considered perfectly kosher where you come from to poke yur nose inty other people's property without askin' permission, but in this country it's the height of bad manners. Now bugger off before I put ma boot up yur arse! (*To Nancy.*) Sorry . . . where were we?

Nancy rips cellophane from new cassette and slams it into DAT. Spanky wanders part of the way across the grass.

Spanky Flip-flop.

Phil *What?*

Spanky You said you was gonna put yur *boot* up ma arse . . . Yur wearin' flip-flops, man.

Phil I am not wearin' bloody *flip-flops*! These ur Thai fishermen's footwear, ya cheeky bastart! (*To Nancy.*) Do these look like bloody flip-flops to you?

Spanky Bye now . . . thanks for yur help, yeh?

Disappears round side of house.

Phil (*calling after him*) Thai fishermen's footwear . . . from Thailand! (*To himself.*) Cheeky bastart!

Nancy (*into DAT*) I'm sitting here on a perfect summer's day with the painter Phil McCann in the wildly romantic garden of the fortified . . .

SPANKY

27

Phil (*overlapping*) What you startin' again fur?

Nancy Oh, God . . .

Spanky reappears round side of house. Nancy covers her face with her hands.

Spanky 'Scuse me, but did I just hear somebody mention the name 'Phil McCann'?

Phil What if they did?

Spanky Naw, it's jist that I used to . . .

Phil/Spanky (*together*) Good God.

Phil	Spanky
I might've guessed . . . Spanky bloody Farrell. I don't believe it . . . Spanky bloody Farrell!	This's so weird, I was just talkin' about you this mornin'! How you doin', man? Jeesus . . . (*Throwing arms around Phil.*) Jeeesus!

Phil God, still the same old Spanky . . . (*Making face.*) What's that yur wearin'? (*Struggling out of bear-hug.*)

Spanky (*glancing down at kaftan*) Doll in Topanga made it fur us.

Phil The smell, man, the *smell*.

Spanky What smell? I canny smell nuthin'. (*Sniffs at kaftan.*)

Phil (*pinching nose*) Not yur shurt, yur aftershave. God almighty.

Spanky I'm no' wearin' any aftershave.

Nancy I hate to interrupt, but could I suggest that you two old chums knock it off at this point and pick it up later? Sorry to be quite so brash, but I've got an unbreakable appointment at Television Centre at four and my flight leaves Dalcross at one-fifteen . . . it's at least an hour and forty minutes drive from here.

Spanky (*overlapping*) Entirely ma fault, doll . . . Boy an' I husny saw one another fur . . . Christ, how long is it, Phil?

Phil Not nearly long enough, Spanks.

Spanky Twenty years?

Phil More like thurty, old son. Nineteen seventy-somethin'.

Spanky Seventy-two. Sufferin' God, you don't look a day over . . .

Phil I know. You look even worse than I do. 'S that a facelift yuv had?

Spanky (*hands flying to check behind ears*) Where?

Phil I would ask furra refund if I was you . . . (*To Nancy, who is heading off.*) Where you off to? Ho, come back here!

Nancy has stuffed everything into her bag and is making her way towards side of house to leave.

(*To Spanky.*) Why don't you try an' locate whatsisname? Guy you wur lookin' for when you turned up in the guise of an interloper . . .

Spanky Miles, yeh?

Phil That's him. You an' I'll catch up later on. Come for yur supper.

He leads Nancy back to table.

Spanky That'd be cool . . . Right, I'm off. Let you an' the doll here get on wi' yur thing, yeh? (*To Nancy.*) Keep pluggin' away, sweetheart, whatever it is yur tryin' to get him to buy inty . . . If at furst you don't succeed, yeh? (*To Phil.*) God, it's so good to see you, man . . . Catch you later. So long . . . nice to make yur acquaintance, doll.

Disappears round side of house. Nancy unpacks DAT from bag.

Phil I'm really sorry about that . . . Huvny seen each other since –

Nancy Nineteen seventy-two . . . yeh, I caught that. I was three.

Phil Naw, really?

Spanky (*reappearing*) Huvny got yur number, man.

Phil 'Number Man'? What's that . . . like a *Game Boy*?

Spanky Yur telephone number.

Phil What you wantin' the telephone number for?

Spanky So I can let you know when I'm on ma way.

Phil On yur way where?

Spanky Back here . . . fur supper . . . later on, yeh?

Phil Ah, of course. Naw, sorry, we've never had one put in. Nearest telephone exchange is in Stavanger.

House phone rings.

See you later, old bean . . . Hope you manage to locate Giles. Sorry, *Miles.* (*To house phone.*) I'm comin', dammit!

Disappears into the house. Nancy checks her mobile and places it next to DAT on table. Spanky wanders across.

Spanky D'you think I could use yur cellphone, sweetheart? Sent ma driver away, musta left mines in the motor . . . (*Picking up mobile.*) God, talk about weird coincidences?

Nancy (*miffed*) Really? Chap in the store assured me that was a one-off . . . state of the art. I only got it yesterday.

Spanky (*putting number into mobile*) Bumpin' inty the boy at the back of beyond, I'm talkin' . . . (*Into mobile.*) Yeh, hi . . . I need a number fur Skelbo Castle. Skelbo . . . naw, private members' club, Scottish Highlands, an' if you could hurry it up. I'm in the middle of the jungle here . . . (*Swiping at wasp.*) Get to fuck! (*Into mobile.*) Naw, no' you, operator, the bloody hornet . . . Get, ya bastart! (*Taking off round garden, ducking and weaving.*) Naw. I don't huv anythin' to write with at the moment, d'you think you could . . . ah, yah bugger!

He falls backwards over space-hopper.

(*Into mobile.*) Text it to us, right! Jeesus God, man . . .

He clambers to his feet.

So, how you gettin' on wi' him? Phil, yeh?

Returns mobile to Nancy, brushes himself down.

Nancy You seem to know him pretty well, how d'you get on with him?

Spanky Last time we met up was in a graveyard. Canny fur the life of me recall what I was doin' there but I seem to remember that he was hangin' about waitin' fur his maw . . . No' too sure if she ever turned up. I once seen hur runnin' up the street wi' hur hair on fire an' stabbin' a guy in the throat wi' a machete 'fore he fell backwards through the Co-operative windy onty the brand-new shurts . . . You want to huv seen the mess . . . bloodstains aw down here.

Nancy God.

Spanky Not that we ever got wur shurts from the Co. Doll in Topanga made this fur us . . . feel.

Offers kaftan to be fingered.

Aw this fretwork up here's hand-tooled. Hunner bucks a square inch. Dylan's got one the exact same, only in donkey brown. He got his in Tibet, he was tellin' me. Sweet guy, Bobby . . . sweet guy.

Nancy Is he another friend of yours?

Spanky Not as such, naw. Well, I say that, but we did once share a roadie at the Newport Folk Festival.

Nancy You mean a groupie, no?

Spanky Naw, definitely a *roadie* – the reason I remember is 'cos the guy that was supposed to be roadyin' fur us was hospitalised after fallin' out the plane on the way to –

Nancy stifles a laugh.

Aw, I get it. (*Laughs.*) Wouldny look too good when they roll the credits on this music video wur makin' up here an' that little gem pops up . . . 'He once shared a roadie with etcetera etcetera.' 'S like showin' off, innit? Even if it isny true. Sorry . . . *is*. George Farrell, by the way.

Offers hand to Nancy.

Nancy Nancy Rice . . . hi.

Spanky Good to meet you, Nancy . . . Canny get away wi' takin' you fur Chrissie . . . thur's a definite crossover there. Naw, straight up. What ur you . . . early forties, thereabouts? Naw, yur lookin' real good, don't get me wrong . . .

Nancy I'll be thirty-three next birthday.

Spanky Ah, there you go, well. That's how come yur lookin' good fur somebody in thur early forties. God. I remember when I was thirty-three . . .

Nancy You couldn't possibly.

Spanky (*oblivious*) We had two albums in the American Top One Hundred an' a single on the Billboard Chart at Number Fourteen with a bullet.

Nancy Pity you didn't shoot yourself with it.

Spanky Yeh, they wur great times . . . What am I talkin' about, they wur *terrific* times! What is it they say? 'If you can remember the sixties you wurny there,' yeh? Well, we wur there, sweetheart, an' I can remember quite a lot . . . naw, not quite a lot, I can remember *everythin'*.

Nancy Oh, God.

Spanky Okay, nearly everythin' . . . one or two chemical weekends I still don't huv a positive handle on, but apart from that . . .

Nancy You've got total recall, yes?

Spanky I remember one time we wur on the road wi' Smokey Robinson an' the Miracles who wur openin' fur the Stones in Toronto an' we all went to this bar in downtown whatsitsname . . . naw, I tell a lie, it wasny Smokey, it was . . . hold on, hold on . . .

Nancy Shit, look at the time . . . how much longer d'you suppose he'll be? He's been on that call for ages.

Spanky Wasny Hendrix, he'd huv been a goner by that time . . . Clapton, mebbe? Naw, that was in downtown Detroit in seventy-five . . . or was it seventy-six? Naw, seventy-five . . . I remember distinctly now 'cos I was jist outta rehab an' I had this *gallstone* that was givin' us merry gyp whenever I done ma duckwalk . . . (*Going into his version of Chuck Berry duckwalk.*) Anyhow, there we all were in this poky wee bar in downtown Nowheresville. I'm sittin' here. Smokey's sittin' across the table from us . . . Christ knows where the Miracles are . . . through in a back room somewhere gettin' zonked out thur gourds, I expect . . . when in walks guess-who?

Nancy (*stuffing everything into her bag*) Tell your chum
I had to go . . . (*Into mobile.*) Message for Barbara . . .
Hi, I'm setting off for the airport. It's now . . . (*Checking
watch.*) Bugger, bloody thing's stopped.

Spanky Go on, huv a guess, you'll never get it. D'you
want a clue?

Nancy (*into mobile*) When you pick this message up,
could you give Sue at the *Arena* office a ring? I may have
to go Inverness–Newcastle and pick up the London flight
there.

Spanky (*pulling kaftan over his head*) Woof! Woof!
Woof!

Nancy (*into mobile*) Tell her I'm on my way . . . Oh, and
Barbara? (*Disappearing round side of house.*) Hunt
through the archive and dig out something with Phil
McCann on it . . .

Spanky (*head still covered*) D'you give in?

Nancy (*off*) Any old crap'll do. I'll ring you from the car.

Spanky (*poking head out*) Three Dog Night! (*Blinking,
looks around.*) Where's she went to? (*Loudly.*) Only one
of the biggest bands in the entire universe at the time!
(*Calling round side of house.*) Drank wurselfs back inty
rehab that night . . . it was fuckin' wonderful!

Phil appears from house.

Phil What was? Where's what-d'you-cry-hur? She's no'
away, is she?

Spanky You remember Three Dog Night, don't you?

Phil Course I do . . . went to see them at the Kelvin Hall
Circus one year . . . poodle act, yeh? (*Crossing to side of
house; loudly.*) Ho! Get you back here, I was only on the
bloody phone to Thames an' Hudson fur two seconds!

Sound of car revving up out front.

Spanky Bugger, she's went an' took hur cell with hur. Doll was textin' us the number, dammit.

Phil I can let you have the number . . . if it's yur memoirs yur wantin' published, you'd be better off wi' Weidenfeld an' Nicolson, Thames an' Hudson're more yur big coffee-table art books . . . Jackson Pollock, Lucian Freud . . . *me*, mebbe.

Spanky Skelbo Castle number.

Phil Ah, discovered where yur missin' colleague's stayin'? Good man.

Takes Spanky by arm and points him round side of house.

Turn left at the front gate . . . A9's about two hundred yards in front of you, you can flag down a taxi . . . Skelbo's just a few miles further north. See, there you go, you're lookin' fur *Miles* an' where he's stayin' is just a few . . . 'S up? You no' got enough for the fare? (*Delving into trouser pocket.*)

Spanky It's me that's stayin' at Skelbo, I'm supposed to be meetin' up wi' him an' the crew . . .

Phil *Crew?* What you doin', goin' furra sail? Not too sure about that, Spanks . . . D'you not remember thon time we went to see *Cockleshell Heroes* at the Bug Hut an' you wur seasick inty yur balaclava? Still, it's entirely up to you . . . *Bon voyage.*

He gives Spanky a shove round side of house.

Remember, it's left at the gate, A9's straight ahead, canny miss it. Don't, whatever you do, turn right or you're on the road to nowhere . . . Sound familiar? Bye.

Phil heads back across grass. Spanky reappears.

Spanky You wur always the bloody same, you couldny wait to get shot of us . . . You wur like that in thon cemetery when we wur waitin' fur yur Old Dear an' she never showed up, only the reason you wanted rid of me that time was because you wur hell bent on fuckin' ma wife, right?

Phil stops in his tracks, turns to face Spanky.

Which you did do . . . on top of Agnes Ritchie Roberts, 'Sorely Missed'. How could you do that, Phil?

Phil C'mon, the wumman was dead, fur God's sake.

Spanky You know what I mean! Cut it out!

Phil Quit shoutin' at us. I married yur bloody wife, didn't I?

Spanky Aye, eventually. Wasny till she told us she was expectin' an' I knew it couldny've been mines . . . What wur the pair of you gonny do, carry on as normal? You an' me wur pals, ya cunt!

Phil We still are pals . . . I'm just after invitin' you fur yur supper.

Spanky Do you have any idea how painful aw that business was? We had a wee lassie, for Christ's sake . . .

Phil I know you did.

Spanky D'you have any notion – any *inkling* – of what I went through? She was Lindy's mother and ma wife, Phil. Ma *wife*, man.

Phil Mine too. And we had a son that I never see . . . huvny seen in twenty years . . . d'you know how painful that is? Any *inkling* of just how fuckin' painful that is?

Spanky I was in the same boat . . . I never seen ma daughter fur Christ only knows how long . . . Don't you think that was painful?

36

Phil You don't know what pain is, Farrell.

Spanky Aw, I know awright. I know what pain is, pal. You don't huv a personal monopoly on pain, McCann. You wait till *you* huv a gallstone.

Phil Wait till I huv a what?

Spanky Aye, you can laugh, but it's no joke, I'm tellin' you. There I was onstage at the Fillmore East just before it shut down an' the boy whatsisname . . . lead guitar wi' thon buncha clowns that hud the chart entry wi' yon rip-off bluesy number whatsisface wrote fur Big Thingwy . . . you know the one I mean? The doll wi' the bad teeth done a cover of it fur Alan what-d'you-cry-him's label . . . the one wi' the big green starin' eye on it, naw? You musta seen it . . . Anyhow, doesny matter . . . where was I? Aw, aye, onstage at the Fillmore West swappin' riffs wi' the boy I'm jist after tellin' you about, an' he's got his Les Paul like thon – (*taking up guitar stance*) – an' I'm on the Flyin' Vee like . . . What'm I talkin' about? It wasny the Flyin' Vee 'cos the roadie we hud snapped the neck off the fucker tryin' to knock a nail inty wur dressin' room wall in Montreal – or was it Vancouver? Anyhow, I'm jist about to take off inty ma duckwalk which you, of course, huv never seen us doin', right? It's somethin' else, man, no shit . . . y' ready?

About to demonstrate – has change of heart.

Naw, fuck, what'm I playin' at? You can see that on wur *Greatest Hits* DVD, drop it inty you later on . . . The nub of how come I'm tellin' you aw this is that I take off in this direction, yeh? I mean, wuv rehearsed it umpteen times at the sound check, only this fuckin' numbskull husny a clue what's happenin' on account of how he's been gobblin' Christ knows how many pharmaceuticals backstage an' he goes like yon wi' his Hofner twelve-string an' I goes like yon wi' ma Flyin' Vee straight off

37

the fuckin' stage an' inty the fuckin' pit, man! Next thing I know, I'm gettin' trundled inty the whatsitsname like thon . . . I'm in fuckin' agony, no kiddin' . . . Unforgettable, it was . . . un-fucking-forgettable. (*Slight pause.*) Sorry, what wur we talkin' about again? Naw, gallstones, right? Childburth husny a bloody look-in. I've spoke to Lucille about this . . . givin' burth's no' even in the same ballpark.

Phil When did you speak to Lucille? As far as I was aware, you an' hur hudny seen each other since . . .

Lucille (*off*) Hullo . . . anybody here?

Lucille, still attractive in her late fifties or early sixties, appears round side of house.

Phil What is this, a bloody Mystery Tour stop-off? Away an' tell the bus driver we don't do teas, yur next stop fur the lavatory's John O'Groats.

Spanky What you doin' here?

Lucille Aw, there you are . . . what you doing hiding in somebody's back garden for?

Spanky I wasny hidin', I was talkin' to Phil.

Lucille There was somebody came looking for you while I was having my bath . . . Who did you say you were talking to? I thought for a second there you said . . . Oh, no, it can't be.

Phil Good God.

Lucille Phil McCann??

Phil Lucille . . . Lucille Bentley!

Lucille/Phil (*together*) What in God's name are you doin' here?

Phil I live here.

Lucille (*simultaneously*) I came to find my husband.

38

LUCILLE

Miles

39

Phil Ex-husband . . . we got divorced, remember?

Spanky No' you . . . me.

Phil 'No' you, me' what? She divorced you as well. Must be one of hur other husbands . . . (*To shrubbery*.) Come out, we know yur in there!

Lucille (*admiring the house and garden*) This's quite something . . . You positive you live here, you're not just a burglar? I wouldn't put it past you. Shame about that outside toilet tacked on at the back there, though . . . eh?

Phil I'm sorry, but that 'outside toilet' happens to be an award-winning conversion from an old folks' sun-lounge area.

Lucille Yeh, into what but?

Phil Into ma studio.

Lucille You're not still painting, are you? (*To Spanky*.) Don't you go and get lost again, d'you hear?

Phil Of course I'm still paintin'.

Lucille How come? You couldn't make a go of it when you and I were together . . . (*To Spanky, on the wander*.) Are you listening, George?

Spanky I'm listenin', I'm listenin' . . . he couldny make a go of it when you an' him wur together.

Lucille About gettin' lost, ya eejit.

Phil Well, I'm makin' a go of it now . . . jist had one of the biggest, if not *the* biggest, publishin' houses on the blower . . . an' I don't know if you ever listen to the wireless, naw?

Lucille All the time . . . How, what are they, paintings for the blind?

Phil *Nancy Rice Show* special this Friday . . . wur doin' an interview together.

Lucille Aw, that's nice, who is it youse're interviewing? George over there?

Spanky (*prodding flight case with loafer*) What's this, yur empties from Meals on Wheels?

Phil Don't tell me you've went an' retied the knot wi' that balloon? Or was that just a gag to get me goin'? You're still a good-lookin' doll, Lucille.

Lucille C'mere.

Phil C'mere what?

Lucille Just c'mere.

Phil moves in close.

That isny a wig yur wearin', is it?

Spanky C'mon, break it up . . . You hud yur chance an' you blew it, McCann . . .

He puts his arm round Lucille.

Hur an' I swapped rings at a ceremony in Vegas jist last month there. Show him, sweetheart.

He waves Lucille's hand in Phil's face.

Phil Hate to tell you, old sport, but she's no' wearin' a ring.

Spanky *What?*

Lucille Must've left it on the shelf when I was having my bath. Nobody's goin' to steal it!

Phil (*to Lucille*) How's the boy doin'?

Spanky He's no' a boy any more, he's a grown man and accordin' to his mother here, he's doin' jist dandy. (*To*

Lucille.) C'mon, you, let's hightail it back to the Castle. What's the bettin' yur bloody weddin' ring's up fur grabs on the bloody Shoppin' Channel right now . . .?

He hauls Lucille away.

(*To Phil.*) An' you know how come he's doin' jist dandy? 'Cos he husny clapped eyes on your ugly kisser since he was eight!

Lucille Nine.

Spanky Since he was *nine*. (*To Lucille.*) Shut up contradictin' us an' *c'mon*!

Lucille Ow!

They disappear round side of house. Muffled cursing from Spanky followed by offstage cry from Lucille.

Phil Happy honeymoon, you guys!

Gives sardonic chuckle and wanders off across grass, slumps into chair and lets his head fall back, staring up at clear blue sky. He closes his eyes. Distant offstage argy-bargy between Spanky and Lucille lapses into silence.

Some moments pass. Spanky reappears round side of house, sidles across to Phil.

Spanky I . . . er . . . need to make a phone call.

Some moments pass. Phil slumps in chair, eyes closed.

Stupit bitch sent wur driver away when she got here. I've got to put a call through to the Club, yeh?

Phil (*eyes still closed*) What, St Mary's Boys' Club? I'll be very surprised if yur membership husny lapsed by now, old son.

Spanky Aye, very whimsical . . . Where's yur phone, at the back door there?

42

He starts towards the house.

Phil Thur's one in the kitchen . . . Hang on.

Spanky waits for Phil to catch him up. As Phil draws level he suddenly swings a punch at Spanky.

Spanky Ah, yah bastart!

He tumbles backwards over kiddies' playthings.

Phil That's fur callin' hur a 'stupit bitch'.

Lucille, alerted by her husband's cry, comes tearing round side of house.

Lucille Aw my God, what happened?

Spanky Tripped over ma shoelaces . . . ahyah . . .

Lucille You're wearin' slip-ons, stupit.

Phil We wur havin' a race an' he fell off his space-hopper. I was in the pram.

Lucille You don't say.

She helps Spanky to his feet.

Look at the state of you . . . Honest to God, I can't let you out of ma sight for a second. If it isny weans' toys it's snortin' coke. Have you made that phone call?

Spanky (*clutching his nose*) Give us a bloody chance.

Lucille (*to Phil*) How many kids've you got? They need all this junk to keep theirselves entertained?

Phil Two . . . boy an' a girl. (*To Spanky.*) How's the nose?

Spanky Extremely painful.

Phil Not worse'n childbirth, though?

Lucille (*to Phil*) Have you got a hanky?

Spanky Gonny chuck talkin to him an' talk to me? Look at the good shurt!

Lucille Aw, shut up, it'll come out at the dry cleaners. Gimme that.

Snatches hanky from Phil, spits on it and starts dabbing at Spanky's kaftan.

Spanky Talk sense, you canny huv a garment like this dry-cleaned, it's got to be . . . Sufferin' Christ, yur makin' it worse!

Lucille Och, here . . . do it yurself.

Phil has gathered up space-hopper, doll's pram, etc. and is heading off with them towards his studio.

Phil Don't want you damagin' yurself twice over, do we, old bean? Just gonny dump this lot in that award-winnin' outside toilet of mine . . . well out of harm's way, if you catch ma drift, yeh?

Disappears off. Corky appears round side of house supporting dazed and rubber-legged Nancy, who is holding scarf to her bloody forehead.

Lucille Uh-oh, don't look now, George, but you've just been upstaged in the headbanger stakes. (*To Corky.*) Coo-ee . . . anything we can do to help?

Corky Warm water an' a flannel cloth . . . Cheers. Don't think it's too bad, but you never know . . .

He helps Nancy to chair.

Lucille (*aside, to Spanky*) I was imaginin' somebody a lot more glamorous . . . She looks a right trollop.

Corky (*to Spanky*) She was on hur mobile, didny see us approachin' the junction, shot straight out . . . Cherokee's a total write-off.

Spanky Same wi' ma nose.

Lucille (*heading for house*) I'll have a look and see if there's some brandy or something.

Spanky Yeh, thanks, doll.

Lucille For *hur*, stupit appearance.

Spanky (*to Corky*) Similar incident occurred a coupla years back when our bass player blootered inty an *elk* in his camper van up in Saskatoon . . .

Corky (*loudly, to house*) Gonny get a move on wi' that flannel?

Spanky (*examining Nancy's injury*) All he had was a wee cut like that.

Corky Coupla stitches an' she'll be fine.

Spanky Next mornin' he was stone deed. Hope yur well insured, pal.

As Phil reappears:

Jist tellin' the boy here about wur bass player . . . road accident in Canada . . .

Lucille appears from house with a basin and bottle of rum.

We've got his Fender above wur fireplace back home in the States, haven't we, doll?

Phil (*looking at Lucille, to Spanky*) Would you not be better havin' it in *front* of the fireplace?

Lucille, looking at Phil, wrings out flannel and passes it to Corky.

Spanky (*looking daggers at Lucille looking at Phil*) What?

Phil In case a lumpa coal falls out an' sets yur hearthrug alight, naw?

Spanky His Fender *Bass* – quit tryin' to be comical. Poor guy left a wife an' five kids, the youngest of which was in a wheelchair wi' jist the one testicle.

Corky (*to Lucille*) I'll take that brandy now.

Lucille (*looking away, shoulders shaking*) Navy Rum – it's all I could find.

Passes bottle to Corky.

Phil A hunner an' forty proof. It worked a treat on the wee fulla's warts. She might want a dash of Coke with it, though.

Nancy lets out a groan.

Corky Here, try a slug of this, babe.

Forces rum between Nancy's lips.

Phil (*to Spanky*) So what happened to *hur*, then?

Spanky Boy there smashed inty hur in his –

A jet fighter streaks overhead, blotting out 'Cherokee'.

– Cherokee.

Nancy shoots forward in her chair and spews rum onto grass, head between her knees, retching. Corky passes bottle to Spanky.

Phil Sorry, I didny quite . . .?

Spanky Total write-off, apparently.

Phil What's a total write-off?

Spanky (*downing what little is left of rum*) His . . . Aw Jeesus . . . (*Makes a face.*) His Cherokee.

Phil Gimme that!

Grabs empty bottle from Spanky and launches himself at Corky.

Ya fuckin' lunatic!

Corky/Nancy Waaaaaaaah!

Corky goes down, with Phil pinning him by the throat, the empty rum bottle raised in the air.

Phil What is it you're no' tellin' me, ya bastart? Eh?

Corky (*chokingly*) Aaargh.

Phil *Tell me!*

Didi rounds side of house, stops dead.

Didi Don't, Phil!

Phil half turns towards her.

Don't . . . *Please.*

Phil Where're the kids?

Didi slow on uptake.

The *kids!* Where are they?

Didi Out front in the back of a taxi.

Phil releases Corky, chucks bottle aside and stands upright. Didi crosses grass as Corky gets to his feet, rubbing throat.

Are you okay . . . er, Cooky?

Corky I totalled yur jeep . . . sorry.

Didi You did *what?*

Nancy (*lurching from her seat*) Excuse me, I've got to go and . . . *bwoop* . . . down your . . . *bwoop!*

She reels across towards the house. Spanky approaches Didi.

Spanky Yappin' away inty hur cellphone. Boy here never stood a chance, if you ask me. (*Removes bloody hanky from face. Big smile.*) George Farrell.

He sticks his hand out.

Didi Fuck off.

She turns on her heel and strides off round side of house.

Corky (*taking hold of Spanky's hand, shaking it*) Didny realise . . . Great to meet you, man . . . Naw, really . . . no bullshit. You're up there wi' John Lennon –

Spanky beams modestly.

– and I'm goin' to be shootin' you later on.

Spanky steps back, withdraws his hand.

How's about that furra footnote in the Annals of Rock? 'S like a date wi' Destiny.

Exits at a run. Nancy emerges shakily from house.

Nancy (*into mobile*) Message for Barbara, picking up where I left off . . . The loud bang on that last voicemail was my *bwoop* hitting the *bwoop* . . . Sorry, I'll have to call you . . . *bwooooop*!

She has completed full circle and disappears back into the house. Spanky crosses to Lucille.

Spanky No' too sure if you heard what the weirdo in the goatee jist said to us?

Lucille What, about you being 'up there with Lennon'?

Spanky About takin' a *pot-shot* at us!

Lucille Look at you, yur dead chuffed! I just hope he was serious.

Spanky No way of corroboratin' that, doll . . . Could be he's jist one of they fans that . . . What d'you mean, you hope he was serious?

48

Lucille I was jokin' . . . C'mere.

She pulls Spanky to her and kisses him hard. Spanky breaks away.

Spanky Aw that heavy stuff that jist went down . . . wasny jist about a stupit motor, right?

Lucille Y'see? And there's you thinking your IQ wasny that much bigger than yur inside leg measurement. (*With an eye on Phil.*) Kiss me again.

Spanky (*touching nose*) Naw, it's too painful.

Nancy reappears from house.

Lucille (*fiercely sotto voce*) Kiss me, ya dummy!

She draws Spanky into lengthy embrace with appreciative noises from her and slightly pained ones from him.

Nancy God, how utterly revolting.

Phil Isn't it just.

Without further ado he picks up the basin of water and chucks it over the snogging couple, drenching them.

Spanky/Lucille Waaaaaaaaaah, bugger!

Phil calmly passes empty basin to Nancy and steps back to let her carry the can. Spanky and Lucille stare at one another, then turn to stare in disbelief at Nancy, who stares back at them, then in consternation at the basin she is holding, then at Phil, who tilts his head back to look up at the sky.

A jet fighter screams overhead. Spanky, Lucille, and Nancy all involuntarily duck and look skywards while Phil lowers his gaze and looks across at them.

End of Act One.

49

Act Two

Later that same sunny day. The remains of makeshift lunch on table. Nancy stretched out on grass, apparently asleep, while Spanky has got hold of an old battered guitar.

Assorted bits and pieces of clothing are spread out to dry. Phil, wearing headset, is tinkering with the DAT recorder.

Spanky plays a duet with his recorded self. Phil turns off DAT.

Phil What d'you mean, 'nowadays'? He shuffled off this mortal coil in nineteen sixty-four, ya mug.

Spanky Naw, I know that . . . I'm talkin' in Buddhist terminology.

Phil In what?

Spanky Did I not tell you? I've became a Buddhist.

Phil What you talkin' about, 'I've became a Buddhist'? The last time we met you wur a fuckin' altar boy!

Spanky I've been through numerous lifetimes since them far-off days . . . I mean, Hector could've came back as one of they midgies, fur example . . . (*Swatting hand in front of his face.*) Get, ya wee shitebag!

Phil He'd've a hard job comin' back as anythin' except furra lumpa charcoal . . . He got cremated, Spanks.

Spanky (*swiping at midges*) Who did?

Phil Hector. You travelled up from Bognor wi' a buncha sailorboys . . . Sparklin' Casuals wur openin' a dolphinarium or somesuch. You got there just in time to miss the entire proceedings.

Spanky Where, at the dolphinarium?

Phil At the crematorium, ya clown . . . Plooky Jack Hogg showed up after you did. You an' him wur sportin' these stupit-lookin' blazers. What was that all about?

Spanky I presume it was because him an' I wur goin' on to Hector's house after the crematorium . . . Jacky Boy brung his foldin' pianna . . . we done a coupla Christmas carols fur his Old Dear . . . (*Sings.*) 'Chestnuts roasting on an open fire . . .'

Phil lets out a guffaw. Both he and Spanky dissolve into laughter.

Nancy (*sitting upright*) You two are really sick, d'you know that?

Spanky Butt out, sweetheart, you wurny even born when this guy got murdered.

Nancy Murdered? God, that makes it even worse. (*Getting to her feet.*) If my office phones your landline with the flight times for Inverness–Dublin / Dublin–Stanstead, would you ask them to arrange for me to be collected and delivered to the new rendezvous point that Sue from the *Arena* office has texted to my mobile but which I've somehow managed to delete? I'm going to walk along to the junction and find out if that garage of yours has managed to pick up my car as promised. Chap didn't look all that trustworthy.

Nancy disappears round side of house. Spanky lowers his head. Snuffling noises.

Phil You sound like you've got a touch of the flu, old bean . . . D'you want a Lemsip?

Spanky (*swiping at his eyes*) I'm starin' inty the fuckin' Jaws of Death, a fuckin' Lemsip's no' gonny fuckin' help!

Phil Oh, *pardonnez-moi* . . . didny realise you wur sufferin' the belated after-effects of post-traumatic stress disorder in the wake of the wee guy's incineration, given that you wur only provided wi' a secondhand, and quite possibly flawed, account of what happened when the pygmy-sized coffin was conveyed inty the furnace.

Spanky Fuck's sake, fifty-nine . . . who woulda believed it?

Phil Certainly not his maw – he was only forty-two when he died.

Spanky I'm no' talkin' about Hector, I'm talkin' about me . . . *me*! Fifty-*nine*, Phil.

Phil turns away, spluttering.

I'm are so fifty-nine, cut it out!

Phil Aye, aye, fine . . . What is it, cancer?

Spanky What?

Phil Quit actin' coy, you've been to the quack fur a check-up and he's told you it's the Big C . . . Long've you got?

Spanky What the hell you talkin' about??

Phil Months? Weeks? Days? *Days.* Wur talkin' days, right? Was it Lucille's idea?

Spanky Was what Lucille's idea?

Phil I thought it was odd, you an' hur turnin' up out the blue like that . . . Musta been a hot-shot detective agency she hired. I've not even got a National Insurance number.

Spanky Don't flatter yurself, buddy boy, if we hadda knew where to find you we'd've been doin' this DVD at the other end of the country, believe me.

Phil You're only sayin' that 'cos you've been sussed out. What was the idea, anyhow? Visit some of yur old cronies and get them to say nice stuff about you on camera, then ask the Great Unwashed to phone in wi' sufficient pledges to provide you with a Celebrity Send-Off? (*TV announcer's voice.*) 'Join us after the break for the Grand Final of *I'm a Has-Been with Cancer, Help Pay for My Funeral!*'

Corky appears.

What *you* doin' back here?

Corky surveys leftover lunch.

Corky Is this your idea of a joke?

Spanky Ho, see when you said 'up there wi' Lennon' wur you meanin' '*up* there' or 'up *there*'? (*Casting his gaze heavenwards on second 'up there'.*)

Corky (*to Phil*) You know that you're legally obliged to provide location catering, and that said catering 'should be of a standard and character corresponding to the religious, cultural and dietary requirements of the production crew' – i.e., yours truly. It's in the contract you signed, or don't you remember?

Phil The only contract I'm signin' is to have you put down, pal.

Spanky Shit, nearly furgot . . . Big Eddie sends his regards . . . (*To Corky.*) Eddie Steeples of Steeples Entertainment Inc. . . . said if I ever bumped inty the boy here to pass on his regards . . . Not that I'm still on his books. When I broke up the band in the late eighties they went wi' Entertainment Inc. an' I went into rehab. Only fur real this time. Got pally wi' this Armenian boy that was comin' off scag . . . used to handle yur top European protest singers, this dude. Guys like Jacques what-d'you-cry-him . . . him that was *Alive And Well and Living in Wherever-the-Hell-it-Was* . . . (*Sings.*) 'There once was a windmill in old Amsterdam . . .' (*Etc.*)

Lucille appears from house, carrying a large tray and dressed in Didi's cast-offs, which are at once too young and do not fit properly.

Lucille Hands up who wants prunes an' custard and who wants . . . (*Spotting Corky.*) Aw, hi, wasny expectin' to see you again. D'you want a Mr Men pokey hat?

Crosses to table and starts clearing away dishes etc. Spanky carries on giving out with the Ronnie Hilton ditty.

Gonny give that a by, George? (*To Corky.*) Bring you out a piece of sausage . . . unless of course you've already eaten.

Corky No' got nothin' vegetarian, naw?

Lucille I'll stick a coupla lettuce leafs on the top an' leave it open, how's that?

Corky sticks roll-up in his mouth and pats his pockets.

Corky Anybody got a match?

Phil Here . . . catch.

Chucks Corky's lighter. Corky catches it.

Corky Ha! My lucky Zippo!

Phil Wouldny bank on it, kiddo. You need a hand wi' that tray, gorgeous?

Lucille I'll manage.

Corky tries lighter without success. Tries again. Still no luck. Lucille staggers off to house with fully laden tray.

Phil (*to Spanky*) You do know that you're referred to in these parts as 'the has-been wi' the acoustic', don't you?

Spanky (*breaking off mid-strum*) Eh?

Corky C'mon, that's below the belt.

Phil And shaggin' another man's wife isny, is that it?

Spanky That is *definitely* below the belt, whatever way you look at it.

Phil Watch it, Farrell, thur's some things that just urny funny.

Spanky Well, I wasny exactly laughin' maself to sleep aw them years back, either!

Phil (*rounding on Corky*) What'd you say?

Corky What?

Phil You jist said somethin' . . . what was it? (*Rounding on Spanky.*) And you can chuck laughin' as well!

Spanky I was blowin' ma bloody nose inty ma hanky. Look if you don't believe us!

Phil What you talkin' about, 'inty ma hanky'? That's *ma* bloody hanky!

Corky Hey, c'mon, you guys, cool it . . . Jist keep it cool, yeh?

Phil One more 'cool it' from you, kiddo, an' yur fuckin' dead, right?

The silence that ensues as Phil and Corky eyeball one another could be cut with a knife – or an old familiar song.

Spanky (*sings softly*) 'Your eyes are the eyes of a woman in love, and, oh, how they give you away . . .'

Phil (*overlapping*) Will you shut the fuck up, Farrell?

Spanky I was jist doin' thon number that . . .

Phil Well, don't . . . just don't! An' chuck talkin' about him, right?

Spanky Talkin' about who?

Phil You know fine well who, quit actin' it!

A few moments' silence.

Spanky Hector, yeh?

Phil You mention that name one more time and . . .

Spanky (*putting hand up to silence him*) Hold it, hold it. You know what you should go in fur, Phil? Naw, check it out, I'm serious. Anger management. Look at the face . . . Listen, somebody like you would derive very great benefit from doin' so. Look at you, yur waverin'. Thur's a joint in the Everglades next door to where me an' Lucille went on the last leg of wur honeymoon . . . Boy was in the Marine Corps in Vietnam . . . What you eyeballin' us like that fur? It worked fur me . . . Soon as you start to lose it they tie you to a log, float you downstream, an' get half-a-dozen Seminole Indians to kick fuck out of you. See, the next time you go to lose the rag . . .

Lucille reappears from house with sandwich.

Lucille One piece on sausage comin' up!

Spanky Twelve Angry Men, it's cried, only you're the one that's playin' Hank Fonda. Do you the world of good, so it would . . . I can let you huv thur phone number.

Lucille registers a certain sang-froid between Phil and Spanky, but says nothing.

Lucille (*to Corky*) Here . . . grab that.

Hands over sandwich. Corky has a look inside.

Corky No' got any mustard, naw?

Phil Naw, we don't. (*To Lucille.*) Doesny say anythin' in yur agreement about havin' to lay on relishes an' suchlike, does it?

Lucille Lemme ask George. (*To Spanky*.) Any mention in our pre-nuptial agreement with regard to 'relishes' and . . . (*To Phil*.) Sorry, what was the other thing?

Phil For the video . . . you must've signed a contract, yes?

Lucille Naw, we just gave wur camera to the guy in the Elvis jump-suit an' asked him if he wouldny mind gettin' us comin' up the aisle . . . Farrell there kept cowpin' over in his cowboy boots so we've never seriously thought about screenin' it for family an' friends. Or is that not what yur referrin' to? It's okay. I can tell from yur face it isny . . . (*To Corky*.) Lemme get you some mustard fur that.

> *She retraces her steps. Didi appears from side of house.*

Didi We have to talk.

Phil What about?

Didi I was going to suggest going indoors, but I can tell from your tone you're not prepared to be accommodating, so . . . (*She turns to go*.)

Phil I am perfectly prepared to be accommodating. Whatever it is you feel you have to get off your chest, get on with it . . . The hippy there's not goin' to learn anythin' new and ma best pal from way back and I don't have any secrets, so fire away. (*Pause*.) Unless, of course, thur's a whole string of other guys you don't want *lover boy* here to know about, in which case . . .

Didi Oh, shut up. Just shut up and listen for a change. (*To Corky*.) Stay put, I want you to hear this too. (*To Spanky*.) You're free to go any time.

Spanky Like yur man said, me an' him's best pals from way back. Carry on.

Didi (*to Phil*) I've had it with this set-up . . . and I don't mean right now, although this's really bizarre, I have to say. You and I . . . are you listening? Absolutely up to here! Not only do you put me down to that bitch from the radio but you really get off with ridiculing me in front of the children and the few friends I've ever invited up here to my house . . . yes, *my* house – *mine* – paid for out of money from *my* work . . . the work that you pass judgement on and never, ever look at! What gives you the right to be critical . . . no, *not* critical, *dismissive* about everything I do, from video installations to that latest commission for a war memorial in Dresden I heard you scoffing about over the telephone to my gallerist. Of all the bloody nerve! And don't deny it, she actually had to ask me who it was that picked up the receiver, she couldn't believe it – she thought you were some bloody delivery man dropping something off at the house!

Phil Even if I was a bloody delivery man, I'd still've said the same thing, only I mebbe wouldn't've been quite so polite about it!

Didi *Polite?* You were fucking *obnoxious*, Phil!

Phil What d'you mean, '*obnoxious*'? All I said was, 'A china shepherdess scaled up to twenty metres high an' clutchin' a sacrificial lamb in one hand and a Lancaster bomber in the other does not, in my humble opinion, constitute a fitting cenotaph . . .' I mean, it's not like her protégée was even goin' to fashion the maquette, never mind make the bloody china doll – that was gettin' farmed out to some poor bugger in the Potteries wi' the know-how an' a 'Sorry, pal, the only credits on this one are the artist in big Roman letterin' along the base of the plinth, an' a separate rug in leftover felt on which the individual names of those carpet-bombed by the British will be embroidered in Gothic script this big'.

Didi That was purely a digital image on a screen, you idiot. There were a number of options . . . and, anyway, I wouldn't expect someone of your generation to embrace the sort of irony that artists of my generation employ . . .

Phil Well, the fact that not one of your generation can draw to save yur bloody lives has to be the ultimate irony, given that you all talk about yurselves as bloody 'artists' . . . that much I can embrace.

Didi Oh, for God's sake, it's the twenty-first century! It's not about drawing per se, it's about making a statement, drawing conclusions . . . not a bloody artefact to stick in a frame! You and that mob of feeble-minded retards from the RSA, with your 'ma knob's bigger'n yours' mind set, contribute sweet fuck-all to the current discourse on contemporary work. The world's changed, and the art world along with it, which is why there are more and more *women* making their mark, and that really bugs you, doesn't it? Particularly when one of them happens to be the 'big ride' you share this house with. It's not video art, installation art, or even the dread conceptual art that riles you, Phil – it's the thought of *me*, unlike that *sainted* mother of yours, creating a stir in that world and, for better or worse, in *this* world that you affect to despise but in actual fact are afraid of!

Phil You leave ma 'sainted' bloody mother out of this! And don't flatter yurself inty thinkin' this's *personal*, 'cos it isny! It just so happens that you and yur cronies don't fuckin' get it, right? And before you ask me what I mean by that, let me *contextualise* it for you . . . Yur a buncha stupit *cunts*! Always were, always will be! Show you a stick an' sure as eggs is eggs you'll grab hold of the wrong fuckin' end of it! You don't understand *anythin'* – language . . . culture . . . art . . . nuance. *Irony* to you lot's like a *baseball bat* is to a *bouncer*! As for *nuance* . . . you don't even know how to fuckin' spell it! You take a

throwaway line – a *bagatelle*, a piece of *gossamer* – and
you cast it in reinforced *concrete*, for Christ's sake! The
size of a house. Then, as if that wasny *lumpen* enough,
you get another silly cunt to screw up bitsa paper an'
sellotape them to the walls of this colossal *conceit* . . .
this hollow *artefact* . . . compared to which, 'ma knob's
bigger'n yours' sounds like a quote from the Wit and
Wisdom of fuckin' Sophocles!

Didi (*to Corky*) Gimme a call later. Bye.

> *She disappears off round side of house. A long and
> awkward silence ensues. It is eventually broken by
> Corky.*

Corky Did I ever mention that I used to play in a tribute
band? 'The Sparklin' Casualties' . . . Kept goin' fur about
eight or nine months. Done a few gigs here an' there . . .
Largs, Troon, Ardrossan, Dunoon . . . then it was straight
down the toilet. (*Pause.*) Miles sends his apologies, by the
way.

Spanky Sorry . . . you talkin' to me?

Corky Had to zip over to Oslo at short notice, asked me
to acquire the definitive list of numbers off you.

Spanky Musical numbers, we talkin'?

Corky You know it's now a two-hour special fur MTV,
yeh?

Spanky It isny, is it? Naw, I mean, yeh, that's cool.

Corky Furst half it's you an' the Casuals . . .

Spanky Naw, look, when I said it was cool . . .

Corky Miles's got about forty hours of uncut live footage
we can pillage –

Spanky Ah. Thought furra minute that buncha tubes wur
aw gonny turn up here. Phew!

Corky – different venues, you an' the band, most of it shot in the States . . . one or two European gigs plus the famous one you done behind the Iron Curtain aw them years back . . .

Spanky Red Square wi' what's-thur-name . . . Nazareth? Jeesus God, never realised they got that on film. You want to've been there, Phil . . . it was like the Second Coming, no shit!

Corky Then it's jist you . . . live on tape. We'll shoot aw that here or hereabouts. How d'you get on wi' the people at Skelmo?

Phil (*sotto voce*) *Bo*, ya eejit!

Spanky Aye, awright . . . How?

Corky Miles wants me to grab some mockumentary footage fur cuttin' inty the second-half songs . . . you an' the little lady gettin' inty all that huntin' shootin' fishin' crap. D'you reckon she'd be up fur that?

Phil C'mon, George, you an' the missus *aping* yur betters? Right up your street, old chum – the deerstalker an' the cowboy sanshoes . . . powerful combo . . . good TV. Look what it done fur what's-hur-features.

Corky Madonna, right.

Phil Naw, Pat Smythe . . . 'fore your time, Sunny Jim. Hur that done aw thon show-jumpin' malarkey. (*To Spanky.*) Did I not see your maw at twelve o'clock Mass at St Mary's wi' a Pat Smythe headsquare, naw? Christmas Eve, nineteen fifty-seven . . .

Lucille appears from house with squeezy bottle of relish.

Lucille Couldny locate any mustard . . . hunted high an' low . . .

Phil Ask hur now, Spanky boy.

Lucille (*to Corky*) Horseradish okay, yeh? Ask me what?

    Corky takes horseradish sauce and squeezes generous
    dollop onto what remains of his sandwich.

Phil Hubby here wants to give you a starring role in his
upcoming MTV special, don't you, George?

    Corky crams what's left of sandwich into his mouth,
    chews and swallows it. He stands there, squeezy bottle
    in hand, eyes a-pop.

Lucille Aye, that'll be right . . . (*To Corky.*) Don't put
too much of that on yur piece, blow the arse out yur
drainpipes. (*To Phil.*) Did you say 'MTV special'?

    Corky's mobile rings. He sticks it to his ear and tries to
    talk – can't.

(*To Spanky.*) I thought this was for some Saturday-
mornin' children's show? Get you in there and get that
face washed. And change the shirt, it's manky!

    Corky wanders to and fro, croaking into mobile, eyes
    watering.

Phil Aye, *now* . . . wasny manky when he put it on.

Spanky Don't you start . . . (*To Lucille, helping him*
towards house.) Quit shovin' us, I'm goin'.

Corky (*into mobile, with some difficulty*) Naw,
everythin's good here, how was Oslo?

Lucille (*calling after Spanky*) And don't go showing yur
ugly mug back out here till it's spotless, d'you hear?

Corky (*into mobile*) Naw, sorry, man, yur breakin' up . . .
Say again? (*He wanders off round side of house.*)

    Lucille checks her clothes drying on grass, gathers
    them up and heads towards Phil's studio.

Phil Naw, wait, where you goin'? C'mere.

Lucille 'Naw, wait, where you goin', c'mere' what?

Phil Just c'mere, yeh?

Lucille 'Just c'mere' what?

*Phil waits while Lucille walks slowly towards him.
They stand looking at one another. Phil brings a hand
up and places it on Lucille's breast. A lengthy pause.*

I've had a mastectomy . . .

*Phil lets his hand drop to his side. Another pause.
Brings his other hand up and places it on Lucille's
other breast.*

A *double* mastectomy. Last year . . . Memorial Hospital,
Battle Creek . . . Michigan.

Phil 'S that no' where they make the cornflakes, Battle
Creek?

He doesn't take hand away.

Lucille Sorry.

Phil What for? I've never cared that much for cornflakes.

Gathers her. Long kiss.
    *Corky appears from side of house, no longer on
mobile. He spots Phil and Lucille and whips mobile
out, clamps it to his ear while turning away from the
'lovebirds'.*

Corky (*faking mobile conversation*) Naw, er . . . like
I say, Miles, everythin's hunky-dory this end . . .

*Phil and Lucille break off their kiss, stand looking at
each other in silence while Corky paces to and fro
'talking' into mobile. He raises a hand in greeting as
he continues his 'conversation'.*

(*On mobile.*) Sorry, didny quite catch that? Naw. I know wur goin' fur post-synch, but I thought we might get the Big Guy to do a sound check jist so he doesny get too jittery when we . . . Naw, that's okay, Miles . . . Me too . . . Cheers, Miles.

Tucks mobile back into pocket. Big smile to Phil and Lucille.

Miles. Jist touched down at Skelmo Castle, shouldny be too long.

He spots Spanky coming from house.

Uh-oh, don't want to put the wind up you pair, but the gooseberry approacheth. (*A wink.*)

Spanky crosses grass, pulling new top on. Bright green.

Spanky So . . . what d'you think?

Phil Get that off.

Spanky Sleeves're mebbe a tad too short but I can always –

Phil It's one of Deirdre's.

Spanky It's what?

Phil Unless, of course, you're absolutely determined to come across as a bigger arse than usual on TV . . . only in a lassie's blouse, yeh?

Spanky Shit.

Disappears back to house.

Lucille (*loudly*) Don't listen to him, George. I think it's rather fetching!

Corky (*gathering up kaftan*) This's dry.

Lucille Away and give him that.

Corky Hullo . . . y'there? (*Disappearing off.*) I've got yur smock here!

Phil draws Lucille towards him. Their embrace is both passionate and tender by turns.

Nancy (*offstage*) What the bloody hell is going on now?

Phil and Lucille, startled, spring apart. Nancy appears with mobile to ear.

(*Into mobile.*) My PA's already had this conversation with the London end of Music and Arts, and as far as I understood it . . . No, I can't possibly get to the Soho House by five . . . Because I'm right at the top end of the bloody country and I've been involved in a serious road accident, you stupid cow . . . I've alerted Sue at the *Arena* office, I'm now rebooked on the . . . Hullo? Bugger!

Throws mobile to the ground and jumps up and down on it.

Phil I must say yur lookin' the better for that stroll . . . Did yur motor get picked up okay?

Nancy No, but it does have a 'Police Aware' notice superglued to the passenger door, and the windscreen, which had a teeny-weeny hairline crack in the top right-hand corner, is now littering the front seats and most of the roadway where some wandering *bagpiper* has put a fucking brick through it. Aaaaaaargh!

Spanky and Corky appear from house, Spanky skiting the faded but still visible bloodstains on his kaftan front.

Corky C'mon, it's no' like yur gonny be singin' *a capella*, is it?

Positions guitar so that it covers kaftan front.

Spanky I can never remember the words.

Phil Don't look at me, I don't even know how the tune goes . . . (*To Lucille.*) Where you off to?

Lucille (*clutching dry clothes*) I'm going to change, amn't I?

Phil You already have changed.

Lucille So have you.

Phil Yeh?

Lucille I would say so.

Phil Do I look different?

Lucille You look stupit in them flip-flops.

She heads off towards Phil's studio, laughing.

Spanky (*to Nancy*) D'you ever feel yur missin' out on somethin'?

Nancy The entire bloody time, yeh.

Spanky Grab this, kiddo.

He thrusts guitar at Corky.

(*Loudly.*) Lucille?

Hurries back to house. Nancy catches Phil's eye.

Nancy If you're about to ask whether it's been a profitable trip for me, coming all the way up here, I'd have to say that apart from your being initially unhelpful, you then went on to be totally negative, then, having resigned myself to that, I had my car trashed in a freak collision on my way to the airport to catch the only direct London flight of the day, thereby missing a vital meeting with the Head of Music and Arts with a view to my fronting up a six-part *Arena* series on cutting-edge British art at the beginning of the new century, which has already been pre-sold to twenty-seven countries around the world together with a book of the series in four languages which I, as the frontperson, would write, except I'm now scarred for life unless I undergo cosmetic surgery, followed by God-only-knows how many sessions of psychotherapy in order to help me rebuild my life as an arts commentator *and* as a woman, so all-in-all I'm completely fucked.

Phil Yeh, I can see where yur comin' from, but –

Nancy I would also like to add that I sincerely hope that everything in your life goes even more badly wrong and that you end up with some terrible and crippling wasting disease that puts you in a wheelchair for the rest of your days and that the only way out is for you to take your own life but that you find yourself too feeble to do so, in which case I will gladly come all the way back up to this Godforsaken hell-hole and personally remove your shrivelled gonads with a hacksaw and watch you die slowly and in the utmost pain imaginable.

Corky (*strums, sings*) 'Sunshine came softly through ma window today . . .' (*Etc.*)

Catches Phil's eye, stops. His mobile rings.

(*Into mobile.*) Hi . . . Corky Doyle . . .

Nancy drops to her knees and starts hunting around for headset. Lucille reappears from the studio in her own clothes.

Spanky (*offstage, from the house*) Y'there, Mrs *Farrell*?

Lucille (*to Nancy*) It's over there somewhere.

Nancy What is?

Lucille Yur phone . . . is that not what you're lookin' for?

Nancy No, it isn't. (*Carries on searching.*)

Lucille You're welcome.

She makes a face at Nancy's back. Spanky reappears from house, spots Lucille.

Spanky What you doin' out here? Thought you wur in there?

Corky (*breaking off mobile conversation, to Spanky*) Miles wants to know, d'you need anythin' from the Castle?

Spanky (*keeping an eye on Phil and Lucille*) Yeh . . . tell him to bring us ma Gibson Kalamazoo, it's in a hard case under the bed in the Presidential Suite. It's got 'Danger – This Machine Kills Two-Timin' Women and Two-Faced Friends' in freaky letterin' burnt inty the lid. Got it outta hawk shop on Haight Street in nineteen seventy-two fur forty-eight dollars cash . . . Boy threw in a capo an' a copy of *The Whole Earth Catalogue* from nineteen sixty-seven . . . We sent off ten bucks furra teepee. We wur gonny put it up out the back green fur Lindy . . . (*To Lucille.*) D'you remember that?

Lucille What, like a wigwam, you mean?

Spanky (*to Corky*) Lindy was our wee lassie. I've got a snapshot somewhere, hang on . . . (*Delving into back pocket of jeans.*) Wur talkin' nineteen seventy-two, yeh? You are not gonny believe how beautiful she . . . (*Discovering contents of wallet soaking wet.*) Aw, fur fuck's sake.

Holds up stuck-together photographs, scraps, notes etc. Nancy, crawling about on hands and knees, spots headset at Spanky's feet.

Nancy (*holds up missing headset*) Ah-ha!

Spanky Look at these . . . look at them!

Nancy (*glancing at stuck-together photos*) Yeh, very nice.

Spanky What you talkin' about, 'very nice'? Thur aw stuck together, an' you know who it was stuck them together, don't you?

Nancy (*getting to her feet*) I've absolutely no idea.

Spanky *You*, ya dizzy cow! When you flang that pail of bloody water over us!

Nancy It wasn't a pail, it was a *basin*, and it wasn't me that 'flang' it, it was *him*. (*Pointing at Phil.*)

Spanky Don't try an' shift the blame onty . . . (*To Phil.*) It wasny you, was it? (*To Nancy.*) Don't try an' shift the blame onty . . . (*Rounding on Phil.*) It fuckin' was you, wasn't it?

Lucille It never arrived, by the way.

Spanky (*shoving photos under Phil's nose*) Look at the state of these bloody . . . (*Breaks off, to Lucille.*) What never arrived?

Lucille The wigwam.

Spanky It bloody well did arrive . . . You'd already buggered off wi' that bastart! I got chapped up out ma bloody bed to sign fur it, can you believe that? The day after you an' him bugger off wi' ma wee lassie, hur stupit bloody wigwam arrives in the bloody post! Bloody wrapper was aw ripped . . . 'Opened and Re-sealed by HM Customs' – like it was gonny be fulla dope, fur Christ's sake . . . I felt like a bloody criminal! God, talk about *ironical*?

Phil How come?

Spanky 'Cos jist the day before I got a big parcel from Eddie Steeples who was in the holdin' cells at the Bar-L waitin' to go fur trial, an' it *was* fulla dope an he was anxious to offload it onty . . . Stop changin' the subject!

Wur talkin' about you an' ma wife an' wee lassie
buggerin' off and leavin' me to . . .

*Mobile phone goes off. Spanky grabs a handful of
Corky's shirt front.*

Get that off!

Corky snatches mobile from pocket, looks at it.

Corky It's no' mines.

Spanky Whose is it, well?

Nancy Oh, bugger. I bet that's the *Arena* office!

*Phil, Lucille, Corky and Nancy hunt around for
Nancy's mobile.*

Corky Ssshhh . . . listen.

Silence.

It's stopped.

Nancy Buggeration! I hope you all die of cancer!

*She bursts into floods of tears and stomps off round
side of house.*
  *Some moments pass in silence while everybody takes
this in.*

Phil (*to Spanky*) So . . . er, what else was in yur *Whole
Earth Catalogue*? I was after some Hopi ear candles fur
readin' in bed.

Lucille (*linking her arm in Spanky's*) C'mon, let's you
and I go for a nice walk, George . . . (*To Corky.*) Don't
worry, I'll get him back in time for his sound check.

They head off towards the trees stage right.

Spanky (*over shoulder, to Phil*) You huvny heard the last
of this, pal, so don't imagine you huv, right? (*To Lucille.*)
I don't want to go furra nice . . . Oooow!

Phil watches them go. Corky wanders past, mobile to his ear.

Corky (*into mobile*) Hi, Miles, it's me . . . Corky . . . Corky Doyle . . .

Phil Gimme that.

Snatches mobile from Corky's hand.

Corky Ooooow! What d'you think yur . . . ?

Phil launches mobile into the trees. Corky's jaw drops.

Ya bastart . . .

Plunges off into trees in pursuit of precious mobile. Phil watches him go.

(*Offstage.*) Ya bastart! Ahyah!

Phil wanders across the grass, picking up guitar en route. He runs his fingers over the strings, a look almost of contentment on his face.

Phil (*sings quietly*) 'Your eyes are the eyes of a woman in love . . . and, oh, how they give you away . . .'

Miles (*offstage*) Excuse me?

Phil What now? (*Loudly.*) Yes?

Miles, a well set-up young man of around thirty, appears round side of house. He has Nancy on his arm.

Miles I'm looking for my cameraman – chap called Doyle?

Phil Naw, sorry, nobody of that name here. Where'd you find *hur*?

Miles Wandering along the road . . . Is she yours? I think she may be concussed. (*To Nancy.*) D'you know where you are now?

Nancy looks around, slightly woozy.

She's got a rather nasty wound on her forehead . . .
(*Brushing Nancy's hair back.*) Look.

Phil That *is* nasty.

Miles I'm Miles, by the way.

Phil Not the *legendary* Miles . . . I thought you'd be a
good lot *darker* somehow.

Nancy Oh, God, I feel so unwell. No . . . really.

Miles C'mon, let's get you stretched out somewhere . . .
(*To Phil.*) Is this okay with you? You're the only house
for miles around. You don't recognise her, no? Could've
been a hit and run . . . Can we put her in that old
greenhouse over there?

Phil What old greenhouse? Oh, that . . . Yeh, why not?

Miles You grab her feet and I'll . . .

They stretcher her towards the studio.

Mind how you go. Have they set His Nibs up with a
dressing room, d'you know?

Phil 'His Nibs'?

Miles Yeh, we're shooting a music DVD in the grounds.
You don't belong here either, do you? Watch out . . .
table.

*They negotiate their way round the table and carry on
with their good deed of getting Nancy into the studio.*

You're not in the music business yourself, by any chance?
I sort of know your face, don't I? Do I? *Should* I?

Phil I've had it fur a while . . . (*Stumbling.*) Whoops.

Miles Easy does it.

Nancy I'm going to the Soho House.

Miles (*to Nancy, as to a child*) No, the *green*house . . .
I'm going to give Jerry a ring, he's my helicopter pilot,
ask him to bring the chopper back and airlift you to the
nearest hospital . . . (*To Phil.*) Which is where?

Phil Thur's a first-aid hut in Thurso.

Miles Must be somewhere closer, surely? I'll ring Jerry.

*They disappear off, towards the studio. Corky comes
crashing back through the trees, dishevelled and
fuming. He turns this way and that. Miles appears.*

Miles (*into mobile*) Raigmore A&E, Inverness . . .
Thanks, Jerry. Bye. (*Spotting Corky.*) Ah, here you are?
Where the hell've you been? I've been trying to reach
you, all I'm getting is your bloody voicemail.

Phil appears.

Corky I . . . er . . . discovered a coupla nice locations in
the trees there.

Phil Didny happen upon a coupla geriatrics havin' a
knee-tremble in one of them, naw?

Miles (*passing sheet of paper to Corky*) Shot list.

Corky (*handing over grubby note*) Musical numbers.

*Miles casts an eye over musical numbers. Phil casts an
eye over his shoulder.*

Phil Ah . . . 'Two Little Boys'? I like that one.

Miles Where?!

*House phone rings. Phil goes off to answer it, singing
the Rolf Harris ditty as he goes.*

Corky (*checking that Phil has gone into house*) The
reason you couldny get me on ma mobile is because that

nutter grabbed it off me an' lobbed it inty them trees across there . . . I've been through every bush an' every bloody shrub . . . up hill an' down dale . . .

Miles (*pressing 'recall' button his mobile*) It's ringing now . . . What're you waiting for, go and find the bloody thing!

Corky I'd like to see you tryin' to find, it, I've jist put it onty '*vibrate*'.

Miles Hang on . . . (*Into mobile.*) Hullo, who is this?

Spanky appears from the trees, Corky's mobile clamped to his ear. Corky has set about unpacking flight cases.

Spanky (*into mobile*) Never mind 'who's this?', who's that?

Miles (*to Corky*) Somebody's found your phone . . . (*Into mobile.*) Hullo? You still there?

Spanky, unaware that he's talking to Miles, wanders past.

Spanky (*into mobile*) Naw, yur breakin' up, man . . . Hold on . . . (*Toing and froing in attempt to pick up signal.*) You still there? (*Backing into Miles.*) Whoops, sorry, Jim. (*Into mobile.*) Hullo?

Miles Lost the bugger. (*Into mobile.*) Hullo? Hullo?

Spanky (*handing mobile to Corky*) Gonny ask who that is, kiddo? All I'm gettin' is 'Hullo? Hullo?'

Corky (*into mobile*) Hullo, who is this?

Miles (*into mobile*) Miles McCann . . . who's that?

Corky This's Corky . . . (*Catching Miles's eye.*) Doyle. (*Removes mobile from his ear.*)

Spanky Ah, wur whizz-kid director. (*Sticking hand out.*) Good to meet you, Miles. George Farrell, better known as . . .

Lucille (*offstage, coming on*) Aaaaaaaaah!

She races on and throws her arms around Miles's neck.

Miles Oooooow! (*Laughing with delight.*) Why didn't you warn me you were going to be here? Bloody hell!

They hug each other, laughing. Spanky looks on, perplexed.

Spanky Ho! Put hur back where you got hur . . . What you playin' at? Who is this guy? What's goin' down here!

Lucille Cut it out, George . . . This was to be the best man at our wedding, don't you remember?

Spanky Huh?

Miles Hey, I'm sorry. No, I really am . . . I was producing a film documentary on the Human Genome Project for Cal-Tech. They sent me off to Japan for ten days, bumped into an old pal who was shooting a Drambuie commercial out there . . . woke up twenty-four hours later, had to google IMDB to find out what I was working on . . .

Quizzical look from Lucille.

International Movie Data Base . . .

Lucille beams proudly at Spanky. Spanky looks from Lucille to Miles and back again.

Spanky Yur kiddin' . . . It isny, it canny be . . . can it?

Lucille I'm not . . . It can . . . an' it is!

She hugs Miles tight.

Miles God, I remember we used to end up like this when I was a kid . . . except ma hair isny gettin' soakin' wet from yur tears fallin' onty ma napper. I *can't* remember you being this happy . . . or looking this great . . . No, you do . . . you look terrific.

Phil appears from house.

Phil That was ma publishers on the phone. Correction . . . ma *erstwhile* publishers. (*To Spanky.*) Boy was very . . . sorry . . . '*most* apologetic' . . . He thought he was talkin' to hur '*agent*' . . . It's not me they want to do a book about, it's *hur*. Didi. I'm still reelin' from the shock, no kiddin'.

Spanky Well, hang onty yur hat 'cos thur's another one gallopin' up hard on that one's heels. Huv you . . er, said howdy to ma director there, by any chance?

Phil Sure have . . . he helped us dump the lovely Nancy onty a bench in the Helicopter Departures Lounge back there. Didny strike me as bein' too quick on the uptake, the boy.

Spanky Ah . . . chip off the old block, then?

Phil What?

Lucille gives Miles a nudge.

Miles What?

Phil (*to Lucille*) What?

Miles (*to Spanky*) What?

Corky (*into flashing mobile*) *What?!*

Roaring downdraught as helicopter hovers overhead and prepares to land.
Lights.

End of Act Two.

Act Three

*Phil's ramshackle studio. Nancy sits with a rug round
her knees and with her head bandaged. She is wearing a
strange little hat in order to partially cover her bandaged
head.*

*A canvas is set up on an easel facing away from us.
Nancy is dozing. Music coming from house adjacent.*

*Enter Phil, a bunch of brushes in one hand, a toddler's
coffee in the other. Sits down at easel and picks up where
he left off with Nancy's portrait. He works away for
some moments. Nancy opens her eyes.*

Nancy Oh. Damn . . . must've dozed off. (*Tweaks at hat,
trying to cover bandage.*)

Phil Leave it. That's the whole point . . . 'Woman with
Bandaged Head . . . (*His brush zips over the canvas.*)
Number One'.

Nancy 'Number One'? How many more are there in the
pipeline? I can't possibly loll around here for ever. I was
meant to be renegotiating another meeting with the
powers that be at *Arena* two days ago. I wonder if they've
left a message on my . . . (*Recalling lost mobile.*) Bugger.

Phil Relax, boy from the garage is droppin' you off a
courtesy car in the next half an hour.

Nancy I don't want a courtesy car, I want my own car
back with all my personal stuff in it – did you tell him
that?

Phil Garage boy said it'll be at least ten days before they
can source a windscreen furra . . . what is it again?

Nancy A Trabant.

77

Phil See, that's the problem wi' yur old Eastern Bloc bangers . . . touch too cool fur the Frozen North. Turn this way a bit . . . I want to get yur black eye in.

Nancy Oh, Christ . . . don't tell me . . .

Stands up to look at herself in glass.

Phil Siddown!

Nancy complies.

You get up again an' you'll get another one . . . this's a serious business.

Nancy (*barely moving lips*) As opposed to what . . . being a brain surgeon or working for Cancer Research UK?

Phil Of course that's what I mean! What are you, a fuckin' *moron*? Now, sit still, don't move, don't talk, and fur God's sake try an' look like a normal human being wi' a bandaged skull instead of some dozy doll outta fashion magazine modellin' the latest thing in 'après-suicide-bombwear'.

Phil starts painting again. A lengthy silence before the house phone rings. Phil ignores it. It keeps on ringing until he eventually and bad-temperedly downs tools and exits to answer it.

Spanky appears in garden dressed in tweeds, Nancy's lost mobile to his ear. House phone stops. Spanky removes mobile from ear.

Spanky What you doin'? Yur a child of the fifties, Farrell. Get a grip.

Slips mobile into pocket, investigates studio. Spots Nancy inside and locates door into it from garden.

Hi, doll, how's the noggin?

Nancy doesn't recognise him, stares.

Yur *napper . . . nut . . . cranium.* Musta took you fur some kinda celebrity when thon chopper dropped you off at Casualty . . .

Nancy Oh, it's *you* . . .

Spanky Capital bitta gear, innit? (*Showing off poacher's pockets inside jacket.*) Keep yur *quails* in this one . . . an' yur sausage rolls in this one . . . (*Brings out a handful of bite-size sausage rolls.*) Jist broke fur wur afternoon whatsit, grabbed these off the chuck wagon . . . Help yurself.

Nancy makes a face. Spanky casts an eye round studio.

Good thing they kept the old people's convalescent wing on as a going concern . . .

Phil reappears.

Jist admirin' yur stoodio . . . Doll there likened it to a geriatric out-patients' clinic, but I put hur right on that score . . . didn't I, gorgeous?

Nancy (*to Phil*) That wasn't about my *courtesy* car, was it?

Phil ignores her.

The chap fom the *garage . . .?*

Phil What? Naw, naw, it was . . . it was jist somebody makin' an appointment to come an see me. (*Having a gander at Spanky's outfit.*) Right, where were we? (*Picking up brushes.*)

Spanky Aye, awright, chuck starin' at us . . . If you think I look daft, you want to get a loada Lucille in hur get-up. Thuv got hur dolled up in a Fair Isle twin-set, a paira high-heel brogues an' a Sloane Rangers' Celtic supporters scarf . . . (*Peeking at portrait – to Nancy.*) Hate to say it, but he's not doin' you any favours, sweetheart. (*To Phil.*)

79

It *is* meant to be *hur*, yeh? (*To Nancy.*) So, is this you been down the road fur thon TV announcer's job you wur after an' back up again fur yur portrait? (*Seeing look on Nancy's face.*) Ah, right . . . say no more. (*Takes off on wander round.*) No' meanin' to wax philosophical ur nuthin', but life's jist one big disappointment after another, when you think about it . . . Take yours truly, fur example . . . There I was, nineteen . . . hudny even started shavin', an' thur was this doll, musta been about twenty-five or so . . . (*To Phil.*) D'you mind Big Jinty down the Finishin' Department at Stobo's? Big good-lookin' doll wi' slightly buck teeth an' a bum you could toast pancakes offa . . . Naw, sorry, yur workin'. I'll jist park maself over here an' watch you furra bit. (*Settles himself down – makes himself comfy.*) Button ma lip. (*Pause.*) No' say anythin'. (*Pause.*) Jist watch, yeh? (*Pause.*) Stuck us in a *hide* this mornin' . . . showed us how to observe without bein' observed, if you catch ma drift. (*Pause.*) Amazin' how quiet you can be when you huv to. (*Pause.*) Be quiet, that is.

Nancy What'd you mean, 'a bum you could toast pancakes off of'?

Phil Right, that's it! (*Downs brushes. To Nancy.*) When this courtesy car of yours *does* arrive, kindly do me the *courtesy* of buggerin' off in it . . . No goodbyes, no thanks fur puttin' you up fur the last two days an' nights an' huvvin' to listen to you cursin' yur luck *and* me and snivellin' inty yur eiderdown till three an' four in the bloody mornin' . . . (*Taking hold of canvas.*) No abject apologies fur helpin' to write off our as-yet-unpaid-for sole means of transport . . . i.e., one four-by-four Cherokee jeep! No regrets fur maligning both me and ma late-departed mother in the same bloody trailer which you then had the gall to expand inty a two-minute epic of way-out-of-order put-down when you *re*-recorded it out there in that garden . . . an' don't try an' deny it because I heard it for maself on ma headphones when I was taping

the boy there's cover version of Matt Monro's 'Softly
As I Leave You'! And above all, no acknowledgement
whatsoever of the fact that yur totally forgettable
doughball features, along wi' yur *keeker*, yur *stupit hat*,
an' yur *bloody bandage* huv been immortalised on canvas
by *me*, Phil McCann . . . because they huvny!

*He proceeeds to pummel, punch, kick, and stamp up
and down on the portrait of Nancy he's been working
on. Nancy and Spanky watch in silence as he does so.*

*Exit Phil in high dudgeon. A lengthy silence endures
for some little time before Spanky and Nancy dissolve
into uncontrollable but carefully modulated mirth.*

*Phil reappears in doorway. Nancy and Spanky
instantly compose themselves.*

*Phil disappears – Spanky and Nancy give in to their
bottled-up mirth.*

Phil (*offstage*) What d'you mean, what am *I* doin' here?
I'm paintin' somebody's portrait! I thought you an' the
kids hud skedaddled wi' what's-his-name . . . *Kinky?*
(*Reappearing, over shoulder.*) What d'you mean,
'evidence'? What '*evidence*'?

*Phil enters followed by Didi, who has children's
clothes folded over an arm and a journal open in her
hand.*

Didi (*reading from journal*) 'April the nineteenth, 1999.
Another fucking day in Purgatory . . . can't work . . .
couldn't work even if I felt like it, which I don't, *underlined . . .*'

Phil Excuse me, but before you recite any more of that
self-referential drivel, can I point out that we are not
alone?

Didi (*ignoring this*) 'Lucky's father up to his usual
tricks . . . referred to me as a "lazy cunt" in front of
our three-year-old daughter and pulled the plug on the

two-bar electric fire which her papa had brought up on the train and which is the only heating we've got in this bloody great shitheap of a house until my maternity benefit comes through . . .'

Phil (*to Nancy and Spanky*) Lies . . . absolute fantasy. (*To Didi.*) Wish I'd thought to keep a bloody journal!

Didi 'Would go back to part-time teaching like a shot but Lucky's father has decreed – *underlined in red* – that, *quotes,* "No mother of my child *stroke* children will go out to work," so yet another impasse *stroke* bottomless pit . . .'

Phil Gonny wrap it up now, Deirdre? It's *boring* . . . wur *bored*!

Didi 'My *second* bundle of joy, *three exclamation marks*, due in five weeks' time . . . when I will be thirty-one . . . one, two, three, *four exclamation marks*. Feel like an old bag and incapable of imagining what it will be like with another, *underlined*, child in the BGS . . . *Bloody Great Shitheap* . . . without money, *underlined* . . . hope, *underlined* twice . . . or love, *black caps* . . .'

Phil Is that it?

Didi 'PS . . . I hope to God it's a sister, *underlined*, for Lucky, *underlined*, I will name her Last, *underlined*, as in Last Chance, *big black caps underlined* . . . *hole through paper*.' (*Closes journal.*)

Phil You don't want to add a PPS to that? Put three days ago's date on it. 'Oh, and by the way, this morning,' *quote*, 'Silly me! I broke Lucky's father's heart, *big red caps underlined*, followed by one, two, three, four, five, fuck-knows-how-many *exclamation marks*!'

Didi Then I envy you, Phil . . . My heart just gradually turned to *stone*. You couldn't break it with a sledgehammer now.

Phil and Didi eyeball one another. Sound of courtesy car drawing up at front of house. Car horn tootles.

Spanky (*aside, to Nancy*) I think that's yur transport, sweetheart.

Nancy Thank God for that. (*Gathering belongings. To Phil.*) D'you think I could take that with me? That *likeness* you did?

Spanky (*to Phil*) Doll wants to take hur portrait.

Phil *What?*

Spanky Naw, I canny believe it either. (*Collects mangled canvas.*) Not jist want to save up an' go furra big Polaroid, naw?

Car horn outside. Nancy takes mangled canvas from Spanky, dons dark glasses.

Nancy (*to Didi*) I'd like to see you do a piece of work around that . . . the journal, the heart of stone, the sledgehammer. (*To Phil.*) I shall display this heap of shit alongside a can of the genuine article by Manzoni which I've just bought on eBay . . . see which one makes Babs want to throw up into the office wastebasket first. (*Crosses to door, stops. To Didi.*) Good luck with the Turner Prize jury, sweetie.

Car horn tootles.

(*To Phil.*) As for you, why don't you roll away the stone from that *whited sepulchre* you're hiding in and step out into the light? The Shock of the New's already old hat, so don't be afraid. Who knows, it might be a shot in the arm to get out more . . . find out what the next generation're getting up to instead of taking random shots in the dark and shooting yourself in both feet . . . That way you're not even going to manage to stand upright, never mind become a front-runner. Okay, so you're a pain in the arse – me too. Why don't you do the both of us a favour and either drop dead right now or wake up and smell the fucking coffee?!

Car horn tootles, loudly.

I'm coming, dammit!

Exit Nancy with her 'prize'. Phil stirs himself.

Phil Hang on – lemme get you a bitta bubble-wrap fur that!

He chases after Nancy with scabby bit of wrapping. Didi selects a small rabbit and large gonk from garden playthings.

Didi Right, that's me . . . (*She goes to leave – stops.*) Oh, could you give this to your pal?

She hands an envelope to Spanky.

I'm sorry we never got to meet properly . . . What can I say? Hello and goodbye.

Spanky (*taking her hand, sings*) "You say "Hi", I say "Lo", you say "Stop" an' I say "Go go go" . . .' Good luck with the book, by the way.

Didi Which book?

Phil reappears in doorway, clocks rabbit and gonk.

Phil Where you goin' wi' Hecky Boy? That's mines. *And* the gonk.

Didi *Hector* calls him *Mister Bun* and the *gonk* belongs to my daughter. Can I get past?

She pushes her way past Phil.

Thanks.

Phil Don't mention it.

Didi Your friend there's got something for you.

84

She exits.

(*Offstage.*) I've got everything I need . . . Let's go.

Phil stands in the doorway, his back to Spanky, and watches as Didi quits the premises. Some moments elapse.

Phil So whereabouts are you, Spanks?

Spanky I'm right here . . . about six feet behind you an' to yur left. Don't panic, I've come across one or two of these cases when I've been out on tour . . . mostly as a direct result of imbibin' wood alcohol . . .

Phil (*turning to face him*) Whereabouts in yur life, I'm askin'? 'Cos at this precise moment I'm up a gum tree without a paddle, I don't mind tellin' you.

Spanky C'mon, old buddy, you'll be fine . . . You've always been fine. Listen, I'd love to hang on an' huv a good chinwag but . . .

Phil (*barring his way out*) Not so fast, old bean, I've told you where I am, you could at least huv the decency to tell me where –

Spanky (*cutting him off*) Yuv told us bugger-all, ya bastart. The lotty us're up a bloody gum tree, so what else is new?

Phil That's better. Now wur gettin' somewhere, Spanky boy.

Spanky See? There you go . . . the same old Phil. You urny happy till other folk spill thur guts out an' when they do, what happens? Naw, I'll tell you what happens – you make a fuckin' mock of them, that's what happens. Well, not me, old buddy boy! You got off light the other day . . . Don't look at us like that, I know fine well what you an' hur wur up to – *correction*, would've got up to if every two-bit hippy, radio interviewer an' has-been wi' an

85

acoustic hudny been wanderin' to an' fro . . . An' you know how I know? Because she used to huv the exact same effect on me . . . soon as she got within a radius of five feet you jist wanted to grab hur an' fuck hur till it felt like yur eyes wur gonny pop out yur napper an' yur heart was gonny explode inside yur ribcage an' paralyse yur brain so you could stop feelin' the terrible pain of bein' here . . . an' I don't mean here in this ramshackle Furst World War pensioners' cricket pavilion, I mean *here* in this rotten ramshackle dumb arsehole of *existence* . . . right?!

His shoulders start to heave. Phil turns away.

See?! There you go . . . yur off!

Phil (*overcome*) I'm sorry, I canny look at you, Spanks.

Spanky (*almost incoherent with laughter*) I mean, it's no' even as if she could hold a candle to Big Jinty in that department!

Phil (*nearly speechless*) Nor a *pancake*.

This is too much. They clutch hold of one another and collapse into a heap on the floor, choking with laughter until exhaustion sets in and tears take over. They eventually recover themselves.

So what was it she gave you to give to us?

Spanky Who . . . Big Jinty? Like a durty look, you mean?

Phil Deirdre . . . said she gave you somethin'. Wasny a big wadda notes to make up for tormentin' the life out of me fur the last ten years, was it?

Spanky No' too sure . . . hang on . . . (*Produces envelope, runs fingers over it.*) It could be a large cheque. Here.

Phil takes envelope, tears it open.

Phil So how come you wur usin' the past tense?

Spanky Naw, I'm almost positive it was the future indefinite – '*could be* a large cheque'.

Phil (*scanning letter*) It's an eviction order which comes into force as of tomorrow . . . future *definite. (Scrunches letter up.)* Naw . . . when you wur talkin about Lucille. 'She used to huv the exact same effect on me,' quote, unquote . . . past perfect, yeh?

Spanky Aye, that'll be right . . . thurty years of chronic alcoholism, marital infidelity, followed by family breakup followed by restraining orders, two jail terms fur assault an' battery, addiction to heroin, divorce, lawyers' fees, bankruptcy, managerial fuck-ups, lawsuits, rehab, more lawsuits – actual and pending – homelessness, women trouble, band problems, six paternity suits in this country, fourteen in the States, bounced cheques, extradition from the US to fuckin' Panama on a trumped-up drug-traffickin' rap that I strongly suspect wur management, Eddie Steeples, was at the back of, followed by a phoney kidnap an' a flight to Cuba that cost us my entire advance from Capitol Records that went straight inty Eddie's back pocket . . . an' as if aw that wasny bad enough, thur's the *present indicative*! That's where the *real* problems lie . . . an' I'm not talkin' about alcohol or crystal meth or what I'm huvvin' to fork out every month fur child maintenance in order to send five of my alleged offspring through schools an' colleges in Boston, Tulsa, Philadelphia, Oklahoma City an' Battle Creek, Michigan . . . that last one's up fur selection to a private kindergarten that Lucille's on the board of so wur hopin' to pull a few strings there, but who knows? That's where hur an' I bumped inty one another again . . . Was she tellin' you that? When you wur huvvin' aw them *conversations* together . . . Naw? Naw, don't suppose she was. She's went inty hur shell of late . . . that's a big part of wur present-day problems . . . pardon me, *ma* present-day problems. The thing is . . . she's hud . . . how do I put this? She's hud stuff done to hursell. I don't mean *cosmetic* stuff like implants ur that . . . in fact, the exact opposite, if you must know . . . stuff she never let onty us about till we wur on wur honeymoon an' then she didny huv to let on, if you know what I'm sayin'? See, the thing was, when we bumped inty one another after all them years it wasny like the Lucille an' Spanky of yore . . . it was . . . how should I say? It was more formal . . . like, I used to – an' yur no' gonny believe this – I used to ask hur out on a date. See? Yur laughin'. I even brung hur a box of candies one time when I took hur to a movie . . . *Nightmare on Elm Street* . . . it was dead romantic. Sorry, I digress . . . Anyhow, there you have it . . . it was a bombshell, no kiddin'. It's gonny take us . . . correction, it's gonny take *me* quite a lotta time to – what d'they say? – 'come to terms' wi' the situation . . . yeh, that's it . . . come to terms. Jeesus, if only she'd told us what she'd hud done to hursell in the furst place . . .

Phil That would've made a difference, yeh?

Spanky You bet yur life it would. I woulda had to think twice about whether ur not hur an' I . . . (*Realising what he's said – laughs.*) Sorry, I jist said '*twice*'. You don't know why that's comical, but it is. Aw, God . . . (*His laughter turns to tears.*) I feel like a total *jerk*. I *am* a total jerk! I know it's selfish, self-centred, an' fuckin' immature, but I'm a rock star! I canny cope wi' *reality*. The real world's a sick fuckin' joke! Why me? When yuv hud *nine* million sellers, *four* Greatest Hits CDs, an' yur *ma* age, yur meant to huv yur kisser plastered across half-a-dozen double-page spreads in *Hello!* magazine in His an' Hurs matchin' bathrobes! I wish ma maw was still with us. She was the only person that ever understood us! An' even she didny know fuck-all about what made us tick! (*Bawling into lining of tweed bunnet – blowing his* *nose.*) Christ Almighty, look at me . . . I'm *sixty-two* an' I'm greetin' fur ma maw! (*Laughing through tears and snotters.*)

Phil Sixty-*four*, old bean.

Spanky What?

Phil Yur exactly one year younger'n I am.

Miles appears in doorway, knocks courteously on door jamb.

Miles I telephoned earlier.

Spanky Bugger . . . (*Delves into pocket – takes Nancy's phone out.*) I meant to give this to the radio doll . . . (*To Miles.*) She husny drove away, hus she?

He makes to stand up.

Phil (*preventing him*) Stay right where you are, buddy boy, if thur's a firearm gonny be pointed at me I want you to act as a human shield, yeh? (*To Miles.*) You did . . . said there was somethin' you couldn't tell me over the phone.

Miles Didn't *want* to tell you over the phone.

Phil Concernin' yur mother, yeh?

Miles No . . . concernin' *your* mother.

Phil *My* mother?

Miles Ma nanna, yeh.

Phil What you callin' hur yur *nanna* for? She was dead an' buried by the the time you arrived on the scene . . . you didny know the woman. Is this yur mother puttin' you up to this? See, if it is . . .

Nancy's mobile rings.

Spanky Sorry, you guys . . . (*Into mobile.*) I'm afraid there's no one here to take your call at the moment, but if you wish to leave a message, preferably of an optimistic or spiritual nature, please do so after the tone . . . and may you follow in the footsteps of those who have trodden the Path to Enlightenment and sat 'neath the Tree of Knowledge and partaken of its fruits, for it is said that he who knowest not whence Wisdom cometh knowest less than he *knew* he knew already which is naught . . . (*Mimicking ansaphone bleep. To Miles and Phil.*) Look, why don't I leave you to do the old Cat Stevens' father-and-son routine and play catch-up while I make maself scarce, how's that? (*Seeing Phil's expression.*) Okay, okay, I'll hang about, but if you see me down on ma hunkers lookin' like I'm constipated that'll be me *meditatin'* . . . not listenin' to nothin' except fur the silent internal screams of the poor, the hungry, and the misbegotten – right?

He arranges himself in a sitting position on the floor, eyes closed.

Phil (*to Miles*) So? (*Pause.*) C'mon, I've had quite a day already . . . Spill whatever can of worms you've come to spill and let's put a lid on it. (*Pause.*) Well?

Miles Why don't you try sayin', 'Well, *Miles*?'

Phil 'Cos it would stick in ma throat an' choke me! What was up wi' yur baptismal name you couldny keep usin' it?

Miles Because *Tom* McCann was lifted from a shoe advert off the back of all them Yankee mags you and ma stepfather there used to devour when you were growin' up together. It was only when I got to Film School and I was makin' a short about American fifties' comic-book art that the penny dropped. You don't call your only son after a *loafer* unless you want him to follow in his father's footsteps . . . That's when I changed it – I didn't want to be just another one of your jokes, *Dad*.

Phil You weren't just another one of ma jokes!

Miles Too late, Pops. Lemme tell you what I came to tell, then I have to get back on location. You know how much you've capitalised on ma nanna's – sorry, *correction*, your mother's – *insanity*. Wore her *madness* on your sleeve like a badge of *dis*honour that brought you lots of kudos in this 'dumb arsehole of existence' we find ourselves in? And don't say you didny because your sometime wife, *my* mother, showed me the collection of newpaper interviews you've done over the past twenty-odd years to promote your artwork exhibits, and you know what? I'm goin' to release that particular 'millstone' of opportunity from around your scrawny neck. No, it's not *kind* of me at all, so don't get down on your knees too quick . . . just listen up. You ready?

Spanky (*eyes closed*) *Om* . . .

Phil *Shut up!*

Miles Whilst being perfectly well aware that I'm possibly giving more with this hand – (*holding out right hand, closed*) – than I'm taking away with the other – (*holding out left hand, open*) – I couldn't live with myself if I didn't let you in on a little bit of family history. Yours and *mines,* as I've now learnt *not* to say. While I was surfin' the web, lookin' into different bits of data for a film I was makin' for Cal-Tech . . .

Phil As far as I'm aware, none of our family – yours an' *mine* – was ever an alumnus of . . . sorry, where was it you said?

A 'ping' as a message arrives on Nancy's mobile.

(*To Spanky.*) That'll be yur guru lettin' you know that fur the last thirty years you've been barkin' up the wrong Tree of Knowledge, old bean.

He snorts. Miles drops a piece of film into Phil's hand.

What's this . . .? (*Holding it up to the light.*) Some of yur out-takes?

Miles It's a 35-mil slide of our DNA, minus the pasteboard mount, otherwise it wouldny fit inside the lid of thon wee ivory toothpick case belongin' to my great maternal grandfather – i.e., yur maw's da – which happened to be the only item of sentimental value left behind by you . . . apart from a durty comb an' a pair of fluorescent underpants, when you skedaddled an' left the two of us, ma mother an' me, in the fuckin' *shit*. (*Indicating slide.*) That's your DNA in the middle, that's mines underneath, an' that's yur mad mother's *father's* at the top there. I stuck a used toothpick along wi' a shower of dandruff from yur comb inty an envelope an' sent them off to the lab at Cal-Tech . . . They got ma DNA sample off the back of the stamp.

Phil What is aw this pseudo-scientific New Age malarky? From what I can make out, I'm lookin' at three identical – give or take one or two smudges – *barcodes* from bloody Tesco here!

Miles Awright, cut to the chase . . . You are not Philip J. McCann, younger son of Patrick and Annie Rose McCann, but the unfortunate result of an incestuous union between Joseph Corrigan and his eldest daughter, the aforesaid Annie Rose McCann *née* Corrigan . . .

He reclaims the 35 mil slide.

Cheers.

A distant roll of thunder as the sky outside darkens. Corky appears in the doorway.

Corky Not wantin' to rush youse guys, but if we don't shift wur arses an' get back on location wur in serious danger of losin' the light, yeh?

More thunder. Corky disappears from doorway.

Spanky Aw, God . . . (*He struggles upright.*)

Miles (*moving to doorway, to Phil*) Got to get this in the can by nightfall . . . Forecast for the next few days looks pretty bleak. Not too sure what you're up to, but I'm back off to the States to prep ma first feature – low-budget schlock-horror movie with a quasi-documentary-type feel to it. Child's play . . . Trust me, Daddy-o.

He disappears through the doorway. Spanky flips through text messages on Nancy's mobile.

Spanky No harm to the doll, but yuv got to laugh. (*Reading text message.*) 'Sorry, was afraid to leave voicemail as think this could be wrong number. If not and you read this message and are up for it, you've got the job. Sue. P.S. If I do not hear back from you by end of day – N.B. 5 p.m – will presume no longer interested or definitely wrong mo—' (*Mobile goes dead. To Phil.*) Run outta juice . . . Shame, eh? Here . . .

He stuffs mobile into Phil's pocket.

Get yur pal at the garage to charge it up fur you . . . You get a hunner notes' worth of free calls wi' that model. She was a cheeky cow . . . Fuck hur.

Lucille appears in doorway, fetching in stylish countrywear. Phil sinks to the floor.

Lucille (*to Spanky*) I've been sittin' outside in that shootin' brake for the last twenty minutes . . . I've got every clue in the *Telegraph* crossword, including twenty-two across, which turned out to be an anagram for 'bored rigid' . . . Are you comin'?

Spanky I'm comin', I'm comin'. Jist sayin' *arrivederci* to the boy here . . . (*To Phil.*) Naw, naw, don't get back up.

Phil I had no intention of gettin' back up . . . (*To Lucille.*) Yur lookin' *gorgeous*, gorgeous. (*To Spanky.*) Enjoy the rest of the shit . . . *shoot*, sorry.

Spanky Naw, as per usual, you wur right the furst time . . . Look, all I wanted to say was . . . (*Getting choked up again.*)

Lucille Whatever it is, just say it an' get it over with, George.

Phil Quite right . . . Get a move on, Spanks.

Spanky All I wanted to say was, I'm no' gonny go through aw thon phoney palaver about keepin' in touch 'cos I know if we we don't bump inty one another here or hereabouts, wur gonny bump inty one another –

Phil – in the hereafter? Yeh, what a drag that's gonny be.

Spanky – in the States, I was gonny say. Boy wi' your sorta facility could do real swell across there . . .

Phil 'Swell'?

Spanky (*to Lucille*) Don't you think, doll? (*To Phil.*) Naw, straight up . . . Topanga Canyon's fulla low-rise adobe art stores wi' lotsa space in rear where somebody like yurself that's jist lost thur stoodio an' discovered thur maw was *keepin' it in the family*, so to speak . . . (*Catching Lucille's eye.*) What? I'm only tellin' it like it is, if that's the wrong thing to do then so be it. (*To Phil.*) Jist one last thing . . . 'Scuse me a second . . . (*Blows nose noisily into tweed bunnet lining.*) I'm really sorry you never got to see ma duckwalk. (*He breaks down completely.*)

Lucille Aw, fur God's sake.

Phil gets to his feet.

Phil (*to Spanky*) C'mere.

Spanky C'mere what?

Phil (*holding his arms out*) Jist c'mere.

Spanky stumbles across. They embrace.

Now, bugger off before the pair of us start laughin' again.

Spanky (*laughing and crying*) See you sometime, eh?

He pauses in doorway, replaces bunnet on his head, and is gone. We hear him give vent to his emotions from afar. Some moments pass.

Lucille So, you've had that talk? What was it about? I know *he's* not goin' to tell me. What was it?

Phil Oh, this an' that . . . the jail, drug-traffickin' . . .

Lucille (*shocked*) 'Drug-traffickin'?!

Phil Aw that sorta carry-on. Don't tell me he's never thought to mention any of that to you?

Lucille He's only ever spoken to me about Film School and makin' that documentary about the human . . . You're talkin' about George, right?

Phil Of course . . . who you talkin' about?

Lucille Cut it out! That's the kinda thing that sent me off ma bloody head in the first place . . .

Phil Yeh, I'm sorry.

Lucille Have you ever asked yourself . . . no, *really* asked yourself why everything broke up and fell apart and I ended up like yur stupit mother wired up to a generator when all that was wrong with me was that I was only miserably, unbearably unhappy! And the reason why I was miserably, unbearably unhappy was because everything to you was one big joke! *I* was a joke . . . our *marriage* was a joke . . . our only *child* was a bloody joke! Every single thing I cherished was a joke to you, Phil, and as far as I can make out it still is!

Phil I said I was sorry. Me an' him had a conversation. Not exactly laugh-a-minute, but it *was enlightening.*

Lucille I'm not talking about you and him, I'm talking about you and *me.*

Phil I wasn't sure there was a 'you and me'.

Lucille Like the other day, when you put your hand here – (*placing her hand on her breast*) – and I told you what'd happened and you took your hand away, and put your other hand here – (*moving her hand across*) – and left it there . . . and talked about bloody 'cornflakes' . . . Why?

Phil Because that's where the Kellogg's factory is . . . or used to be: Battle Creek, Michigan. The same place that you had . . . (*Stops himself.*)

Lucille The same place that I had what? C'mon, Phil. Say it. Try. Just this once . . . had what?

Phil An uncle . . . yur Uncle Joseph. He sent yur Old Dear a *care* package – coupla boxes of Rice Krispies and a big tin of cling peaches, along with a ballgown which you wore to that year's staff dance. Don't tell me you don't remember, 'cos *I* do.

Lucille That was almost *fifty* years ago and it wasn't *me* that had the Uncle Joseph, it was my pal Bernadette. What *I* remember is being diagnosed eighteen months back and having an operation last year, and that's what I'm living with now . . . *now*, Phil.

Phil And I'm living with the fact that ma poor old demented mother, God rest hur soul, did not spend the best part of hur adult life tied to a rubber mattress with electrodes bolted to hur skull in order to provide hur beloved son with bona-fide fodder for his canvases, but because . . . and this's where . . . (*making an effort*) this's where *Miles* comes into the picture . . . I'm sorry, I'm actually findin' this quite difficult . . . The truth is . . . the truth is that I'm not who I think I am – correction, who I *thought* I was.

Lucille So, who are you? Because you still look and be-have like the rotten bastard that left your nine-and-a-half-year-old son and me to the mercy of the Social

96

Services and blew town with the big tart with the overbite and the huge arse that used to work in the Finishing Dep— What's so bloody comical?

Corky reappears in doorway. Roll of thunder, closer now.

Corky Don't wish to dampen the fire 'twixt you pair of old flames, but yur son, the director, wants you back in the shootin' brake toot sweet, sugar.

Lightning flash. Phil is recovering from the memory of running off with Big Jinty.

Phil (*to Corky*) Give us two minutes. Tell Miles –

Lucille (*cutting Phil off, to Corky*) I'll be right there. (*To Phil.*) Seeing as how I've been unable to catch up with you in the here and now, I'll settle for catching up with you in the hereafter, wherever the hell that is. (*Going around Corky.*)

Phil Naw, wait . . . Lucille?

Lucille Then again, mebbe not, eh?

She disappears off.

Phil Lucille!

Corky bars the way out.

Corky Lucky fur me I can jist zip across country on the quad bike that Skel*mo* lent us, so I don't huv to rush.

Phil (*loudly, after Lucille*) I don't want to wait fur the hereafter!

Corky D'you get that 'order to quit' notice we sent you?

Sound of shooting brake revving up outside.

Phil *Lucille!*

Corky Good . . . 'cos soon as you an' yur garbage ur outta here wur gonny dismantle this feeble erection an' bang up a state-of-the-art workshop-cum-nursery block that'll not only accommodate Didi but the new arrival. Talkin' of which . . .

Nancy has appeared in garden.

What's *she* doin' back here?

He takes hold of Phil's arm and crosses to shout through glass.

Ho! What wur you told, you?

Nancy looks up from mobile search.

No interviews till she gets word about the Big One – right?!

Crashing thunder and lightning.

Christ, I better get ma leg over that quad an' knock this sucker on the head before the *deluge*.

He opens door to garden, shoves Phil outside, and exits via house. Phil takes Nancy's phone from his pocket, holds it up. Nancy strides across and snatches it from him, tries switching it on.

Nancy *Bugger.*

Phil Miss yur train?

Nancy Hit a tractor.

Phil (*singing to himself*) 'Gonna roll away the stone . . .'

Nancy gives him a look.

(*To Nancy.*) Give us a break, it's bloody *monumental* – forty tons of *concrete*. (*Holds arm out.*) C'mon an' I'll fix you somethin' to drink.

Nancy (*linking her arm in his*) As long as it's not that hellish Navy Rum or some of that baby sick you forced on me the other . . . Ooooooooooow!

As a jet fighter screams over.

Phil (*in ensuing silence*) Lemme show you where the house phone is.

Nancy It's okay. After I hit the tractor I careened into the last telephone kiosk this side of Wick. Phoned the chap from the garage – he dropped me off outside the house. Almost got run over by a bloody shooting brake.

Phil Naw, to phone the office – put a call through to what's-hur-name?

Nancy Babs . . . Barbara.

Phil Naw, Sue . . . *Arena.*

Nancy *What?*

Phil Sent you a text jist before yur battery gave out.

Nancy stops dead.

You've got the gig.

Nancy If this's another one of your jokes, I swear to God I'll . . . (*Realising for once that he's not joking.*)

Phil (*sniffing the air*) What's that funny smell . . . D'you smell it?

Nancy (*sniffing*) Don't tell me. It can't be. Can it?

Nancy/Phil (*together*) The fucking *coffee.*

Phil You've got two minutes. Through the studio, into the house, yella door into the kitchen, wall-mounted phone on yur right . . .

He propels her towards the studio.

(*Calling after her.*) Next to the big squared-up charcoal drawin' I done fur Mental Health . . . Canny miss it!

He watches as Nancy races towards studio and disappears through doorway into house. Phil is left alone in the garden with his thoughts.

A few moments later Didi appears in the garden. She walks towards Phil. He turns to look at her.

Didi I brought him back.

Phil Brought who back?

Didi 'Hecky Boy'.

She produces little soft rabbit, offers it to Phil.

Go on . . . take it. Correction, *him*.

Phil (*taking rabbit*) You sure?

Didi It's one of the few things I am sure about.

She turns to leave.

Phil Naw, wait . . .

Didi keeps on going.

Didi?

She stops, turns to face Phil.

If they don't give you the Turner tell the stupit bastarts that I'll be round to huv them measured fur thur throwaway-line overcoats, yeh?

Didi (*wiping eyes, laughing*) I sure will. Thanks.

She disappears off. Lights slowly down as Phil stands alone in the garden. He turns to face away from the house and studio. A flash of lightning picks out Lucille, who appears in the garden behind him. Phil turns. Blackout.

Another lightning flash – longer this time. Lucille in Phil's arms. Blackout.

Curtain.